GLASGOW'S RIVER

GLASGOW'S RIVER

Brian D. Osborne, Iain Quinn and Donald Robertson

LINDSAY
PUBLICATIONS

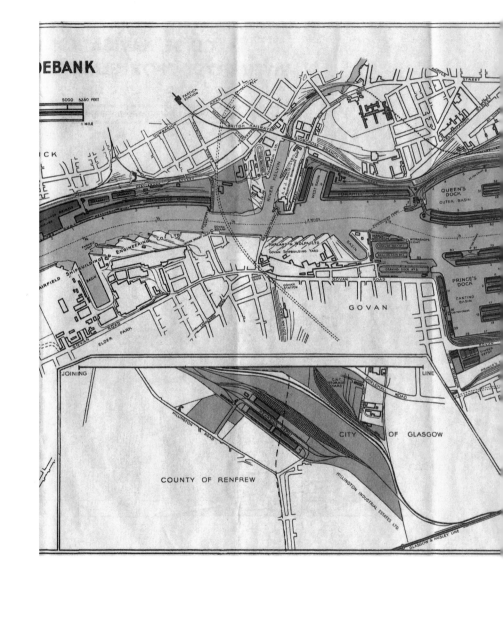

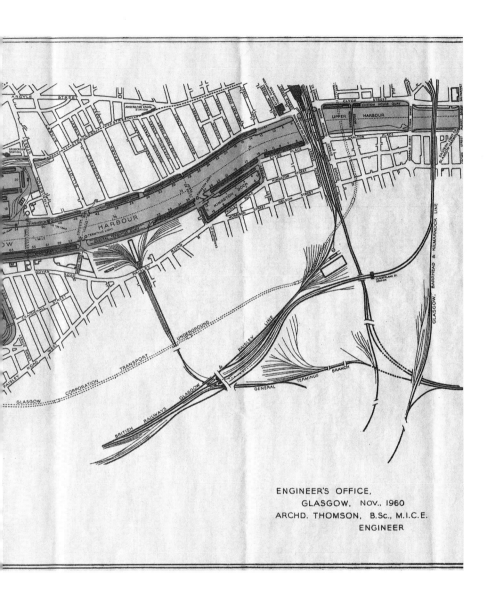

ENGINEER'S OFFICE,
GLASGOW, Nov., 1960
ARCHD. THOMSON, B.Sc., M.I.C.E.
ENGINEER

Glasgow's River from Custom House Quay to Merklands Quay

This edition published in 1996 by
Lindsay Publications
Glasgow

ISBN 1 898169 08 X

A CIP record of this book is available from the British Library

Designed and typeset in 11/13pt Berkeley
by Janet Watson

Reproduction by
Mitchell Graphics, Glasgow.

Front cover: Queen's Dock and Stobcross Quay.
Photo: Hunting Aerofilms Ltd.

Back cover: Looking downriver from the city, showing King George V
bridge, Broomielaw (right) leading to Stobcross Quay and Queen's Dock
(now S.E.C.C.) with Kingston Dock (left) and Bridge Wharf.
Photo: Hunting Aerofilms Ltd.

Title page: "Doon the Watter!" – an early summer morning
on the river in 1937.
Photo: Colin G. Campbell

Printed and bound in Scotland
by Bell & Bain Limited

Foreword

I greatly welcome the opportunity of commending this story of Glasgow's river to all interested in the maritime scene. Early this century Glasgow was the third British port after Liverpool and London in terms of net registered shipping, virtually all of it British shipping. The decline was gradual with various peaks and troughs through the century; the two World wars having their own particular impact on World trade and on shipping in general, but the greatest decline has been over the last forty years. The story captures the Clyde scene as I remember: watching the traffic in the river from the Govan Ferry or from King George V bridge when travelling to and from school in the late 1950's, I would regularly stop my bicycle and watch awe inspired.

Where are all the ships now? Where are all the cargoes and where are all the people that journeyed by sea? The ships are bigger and more specialised, the cargoes are in containers on the roads and the people by and large are in aircraft.

As recently as 1970 the UK merchant fleet was the third largest in the World, amounting to 11% of World tonnage. Today it amounts to just 1%. What an astonishing change for a major island trading nation, so dependent on the sea for its imports and exports. The steamers that plied the river and sailed to and from the resorts of the Firth of Clyde, Ireland and the Western Isles have all disappeared.

Since 1975, I have had the honour to be entrusted with Command of the very last of the Clyde Steamers, the Waverley. As she makes her historic voyages up and down the river each summer, her passengers are entertained with a fine commentary taking them back to the days when the Clyde was not only home to every conceivable type and class of ship trading but was also the leader in the development and construction of the finest ships ever to sail the oceans of the World.

Captain David Neill
(P. S. Waverley)

Acknowledgements

We are grateful to Captain David Neill for providing the foreword to this book. Our thanks also go to Robin B. Boyd; John Ramsay for the use of a number of his photos; Ian Gordon of the Mitchell Library and the Clyde River Steamer Club. Thank you also to Leslie Brown, Dr Joe McKendrick and David Duncanson for reading this manuscript and providing helpful comments. Finally to you the Reader or Passenger on board *Waverley*, we hope you enjoy this view of Glasgow's River.

Note: In the cross headings the symbol

 indicates a site or location on or near the North bank

 indicates a river feature (such as a bridge or ferry)

 a site or location on or near the South bank of the Clyde

R Victoria Bridge

This bridge, which was built in 1851-54 to plans by James Walker of London, is on the site of Glasgow's original river crossing. The first wooden bridge on the site appears to have been built by 1285 and was replaced by a stone bridge, traditionally said to have been erected by Bishop Rae, in 1350. This ancient bridge was twice widened, in 1777 and again in 1821, but proved to be inadequate for the traffic of the growing city.

Victoria Bridge was the starting point for the down river service operated by the Clutha ferries. These small passenger steamers, whose name came from the old poetic title for the River Clyde, were provided by the Clyde Navigation Trust, and ran from their base here in the city centre down river, calling at the Broomielaw, Stobcross (for Queen's Dock), Plantation (for Prince's Dock), Highland Lane, Pointhouse, Meadowside, and Whiteinch. The service began on Easter Saturday, 12th April 1884, with the first ferry sailing from Victoria Bridge at 5.00 a.m. on the down-river journey and the first up-river sailing, from Whiteinch, leaving at 5.40 a.m. A half hourly service was maintained until 8.00 p.m.

The Clutha service lasted for only nineteen years but it won a special place in the city's affections and folklore. The last-ever sailing was made on St. Andrew's Day, 30th November 1903 and was carried out by Clutha No.11. At the peak of the service twelve Cluthas were in commission and many employees in the Clyde's shipyards, engineering works and docks went back and forth to work daily in the Cluthas. The *Glasgow Herald* commented when the service ended:

> For thirteen years they were rather a remarkable financial success bringing to the Clyde Trust an average return of 4%. . . The subways and the railways unquestionably did much to withdraw traffic from the Cluthas but it was unquestionably the electric cars of the Corporation that struck the final blow.

The first four Cluthas, 74 foot long and each accommodating 235 passengers, came from the Rutherglen yard of T. B. Seath & Company, and were followed by two larger boats, 102 foot long and capable of carrying 350 passengers, from the same yard. The Clutha fleet was added to in 1890 by two 80 foot boats from the Dumbarton yard of Murray Brothers. This yard built a further two Cluthas, this time 90 footers capable of carrying 360 passengers, in 1891. The fleet was completed by Cluthas 11 and 12, from the Port Glasgow yard of Russell & Company in 1896.

Clutha No. 7 (1890)

Just how popular and heavily used the Cluthas were is confirmed by the passenger figures for 1887, in that year they attracted over 1,615,000 passengers – a total which was, however, to be considerably exceeded in later years when more ferries came into service. As the *Glasgow Herald* suggests, it was undoubtedly the coming of the city's subway system in 1896 and the completion of the electrification of the very comprehensive network of Glasgow's world-famous tram system in 1901 which made the Cluthas uneconomic and resulted in their being taken out of service after a period of reduced level operations. The *Glasgow Herald* optimistically suggested:

> Perhaps when we have a clean and sweet-smelling Clyde, it will be worthwhile, either for the Corporation or for some enterprising capitalist, to establish a fleet of electric launches by means of which Rutherglen and Paisley may be brought in touch for purposes of business or pleasure.

The Clyde is now clean and sweet-smelling enough but sadly the electric launches are still missing!

The subway system, which did so much to destroy the viability of the Clutha ferries, passes under the Clyde by means of two tunnels. One runs between the Suspension Bridge and Glasgow Bridge, while the other runs between Meadowside and Govan.

Ñ *S.V. Carrick*

This well-known and seemingly permanent piece of cityscape lay below Victoria Bridge for many years. Of composite construction, that is with an iron frame and wooden planking, she was built by William Pile & Hay at Sunderland in 1864 and launched as the *City of Adelaide* for Devitt & Moore's service to Australia. She carried passengers and cargo out to Australia, returning with cargoes of wool, wheat and copper. In a varied career she was a North Atlantic timber ship, an isolation hospital in Southampton before being bought by the Admiralty in 1893 to serve as the drill ship for the Clyde Division of the Royal Naval Volunteer Reserve and was based at the Great Harbour in Greenock. After the Second World War she was no longer required in this role and was bought by the Glasgow R.N.V.R. to serve as their clubhouse and in May 1949 she was towed from Queen's Dock to Custom House Quay. In 1990 she was acquired by the Glasgow Ship Trust and moved to Prince's Dock where she sank at her moorings in February 1991. She was acquired by the Scottish Maritime Museum in January 1992, raised in March and moved to Irvine in May 1992. She is now on a slipway on the former Ayrshire Dockyard site at Irvine where she will, over a lengthy period of time, be restored as the *City of Adelaide*.

Ñ Custom House Quay

Situated between Victoria Bridge and Jamaica St Bridge this quay was frequented by the coasters of J & A Gardner, such as the *Ardachy*, *Ardchattan*, and *Bonawe*, which brought granite from the company's quarries at Bonawe in Argyll to pave the streets of Glasgow. Other bulk building materials, such as sand and gravel, were also brought in to this quay in the heart of the city. A major customer of Gardner's was the Glasgow Corporation Tramways Department who used the granite setts to strengthen their tram lines. A special tramway line was laid into the quay and low-loaders were provided to take materials to the Tramway Department's Coplaw Works in Pollokshields in the South side of the city.

Sir William H. Raeburn (1928). Dredging off Custom House Quay.

The other Gardner's coasters were normally given names of Scottish saints – such as *St. Enoch* and *St. Rule*.

Behind Custom House Quay in Clyde Street were the offices of John Williamson & Company. This firm's white funnelled steamers, such as the *Isle of Arran* and *Eagle III* and later the pioneering turbine *King Edward* of 1901 served *Arran* and the Clyde coast resorts. Further down river, nearer Jamaica Street Bridge, were the berths used by small lighters such as the *Plover* and the *Lintie* which carried general cargoes to and from the Clyde Coast resorts. These berths were also used by coasting vessels such as the *Islandmagee* and the *Olderfleet*.

Carlton Place

Behind Carlton Place on the riverfront lies Carlton Court, the location of the offices of the Clyde Shipping Company, famed as one of the world's oldest shipping companies. Still in existence, this venerable firm's origins date back to 1815 when it acquired the wooden paddle steamers *Industry* and *Trusty*. In later years one of the company's subsidiaries was the Glenlight Shipping Company, the last operator of puffers to the Highlands and Islands.

The puffer was one of the most characteristic and best-loved vessels of the Clyde and evolved from the small iron scows built for service on the Forth and Clyde canal. The puffer, which more formally might be called a steam lighter, gained its popular name from the sound, in the earliest models, of the engine exhaust venting through the funnel. The name stuck even when diesel engined vessels were built. The puffers were built in three sizes depending on the area in which they were to trade, but all shared a broadly similar design with cargo handling facilities and a hull form which allowed them to be beached for loading and discharging cargoes at places where piers and harbour facilities were lacking. The puffers carried anything and everything, grain to island distilleries, coal to Highland villages, and timber, stone and sand from the Highlands for city building projects, farmer's flittings and household furnishings.

The puffer was, of course, to be immortalised in the Para Handy stories of Neil Munro. These originally appeared in the *Glasgow Evening News* between 1905 and 1924 and were also later collected in book form. These tales of Captain Peter Macfarlane, "Para Handy", Dougie the mate, Macphail the engineer and the rest of the crew of the *Vital Spark* – "the smertest boat in the tred" – have also been turned into television series, plays and inspired the popular film *The Maggie*. Munro has Para Handy describe the *Vital Spark*, and indeed the classic puffer, in the very first story:

If you never saw the *Fital Spark*, she is aal hold, with the boiler behind, four men and a derrick, and a watter-butt and a pan-loaf in the fo'c'sle. Oh man! she wass the beauty! She wass chust sublime!

On a Tuesday afternoon in 1935, Clyde Shipping Co's. *Fastnet* is seen passing. Whiteinch on the weekly round trip to Dublin, Waterford and Cork.
Photo: F.A. Plant.

Perhaps one of the most unusual features of the puffer is that the great centre of puffer building was sixteen miles from the nearest salt water. The Dunbartonshire town of Kirkintilloch, on the Forth and Clyde Canal, had two shipyards which specialised in the construction of puffers, launching them sideways into the narrow waters of the canal. As late as the 1930s there were still around sixty puffers trading in the Clyde and West Highland area.

R Suspension Bridge

The suspension bridge was completed in 1853 at a cost of £6,000 and originally pedestrians using it had to pay a half-penny toll for the privilege.

R Jamaica Street Bridge or Glasgow Bridge

This is the third bridge on this site. The first was built to plans by William Mylne of Edinburgh in 1768-71. The bridge we see today replaced the second bridge, built in 1833-35 by Thomas Telford. Telford's seven arched bridge was inconvenient for shipping on the river as well as being too narrow for the city's ever-increasing road traffic. Plans were drawn up for a four arched bridge, which would

Glasgow Bridge in the early 20th Century.
Photo: Strathkelvin District Libraries, MacEwan collection.

have been more convenient for river traffic, but the pressure of public opinion forced a return to a seven arch design and the utilisation of much of the stonework of the original bridge, although otherwise the bridge was larger and stronger. It was completed in 1899, the engineers being Blyth & Westland of Edinburgh.

R Central Station Bridge

In fact there are two bridges here, side by side. Of the first, constructed when the Caledonian Railway built Central Station in 1876-78, only the piers remain. The second was built to accommodate the station extension of 1889-1905 and was designed by Donald Matheson, the Caledonian Railway's engineer and built by Sir William Arrol & Co.

R King George V Bridge

This was built between 1924 and 1927 and the redevelopment of the area resulted in significant changes to passenger and cargo shipping services in the Broomielaw area on the North bank and the Bridge Wharf area on the South bank. The bridge, built in reinforced concrete faced with Scottish granite, was officially dedicated by King George V on 12th July 1927. The new bridge did not prove immediately popular with horse-drawn traffic as the rise to the centre of the bridge was quite steep for horses. One of the design considerations which led to this was the need to provide sufficient clearance for puffers and other small coasting vessels using the quays upstream of the Bridge. On the other hand one advantage of the new bridge was that, for the first time in years, the citizens of Glasgow could get an uninterrupted view of traffic in the upper river.

N Broomielaw

This quayside on the North bank of the river, stretching down-stream from the modern King George V Bridge, had been from the end of the seventeenth century the harbour of Glasgow. Until the deepening of the river in the nineteenth century, however, only the smallest of coasting vessels could get up-river to discharge their cargoes in the city centre. Although there is a report of a 150 ton schooner from Portugal making her way to the Broomielaw in 1806 it was not until 1818 that the first foreign trade vessels could regularly unload in Glasgow rather than at one of the city's down river outports. It was from the Broomielaw that Henry Bell's *Comet*

Isle of Arran (1892) with *Lord of the Isles* (1891) at Broomielaw.

in 1812 inaugurated Europe's first commercial steamer service. By this time the Broomielaw Quay had been extended in length to 900 feet.

The Broomielaw had been the traditional departure point for the river and Irish steamers while the Campbeltown steamers had sailed from Bridge Wharf on the opposite, South, bank. After the new King George V Bridge was opened to traffic in 1928 the river steamer fleet moved their base to the South bank and the Campbeltown boats the *Davaar* and the *Dalriada* took over the Broomielaw berths.

On summer evenings in the late 1920's and early 1930's ship-watchers could have an enjoyable time watching the various ships coming in to their berths – first came the *Columba* turning her 301 foot length to face down-river for the next morning's departure, then followed the Williamson-Buchanan fleet. The evening's entertainment was concluded by the departure of the Irish boats.

Whatever side the down-river steamers departed from there was a long tradition of the Glaswegian going "doon the watter" either for a day's pleasure trip or for a longer holiday visit. The Clyde coast towns had a special relationship with their Glasgow visitors, even if the resorts were perhaps not quite so dependent on them as

Opposite: The *Dalriada* (1926) at Broomielaw, 1934. The dome of the Clyde Trust's building dominates the background.

Neil Munro's irrepressible Glasgow waiter and Kirk beadle, Erchie McPherson, suggests:

> Ye may say whit ye like, I'm shair they shut up a' thae coast toons when us bonny wee Gleska buddies is no' comin' doon wi' oor tin boxes, and cheerin' them up wi' a clog-wallop on the quay.

Elsewhere the same homespun philosopher reports on life at the seaside in the Fair Holidays:

> And it's that homely doon aboot Rothesay and Dunoon, wi' the Gleska wifes hangin' ower the windows tryin' as hard as they can to see the scenery, between the whiles they're fryin' herrin' for Wull.

The writer J. J. Bell, the creator of "Wee MacGreegor", wrote in his 1932 book, *The Glory of Scotland*, of the Clyde steamer services, and his picture of a now-vanished network of rail and steamer services is worth quoting to get something of the flavour of the inter-war period on the Clyde:

> Besides the fleets of the railway companies, there are the Williamson steamers and the long-famous MacBrayne's *Columba*. Most of them have their regular daily sailings, short or whole-day trips; some have different excursions for certain days of the week. The railway steamers start from the companies' piers, all about an hour's train journey from Glasgow, at Craigendoran, Greenock, Gourock, Wemyss Bay, Fairlie and Ardrossan. Certain of the Williamson steamers and MacBrayne's *Columba* sail from Glasgow, and connect with trains at Greenock and Gourock. Many of the steamers make evening cruises and Sunday excursions.

Changed days indeed!

One distinctive feature of the Clyde steamer sailings which Bell did not mention was the on-board musical entertainment. In the days before the First World War the railway steamers had traditionally carried a German band – and in the spy scares and jingoistic sentiment of the period these innocent musicians were sometimes looked upon with suspicion. The crew of the *Vital Spark* discussed the problem of German spies and steamer musicians. Dougie, the mate points out:

> "The country's overrun wi' Chermans. . . You've seen hunders o' them though you maybe didna ken. They're Chermans that plays the bands on the river steamers.""Are they? are they?" said Para

Handy with surprise, "I always thought yon chaps wass riveters, or brassfeenishers, that chust made a chump on board the boat wi' their instruments when she wass passin' Yoker and the purser's back wass turned." "Germans to a man!" said Sunny Jim. "There's no a Scotchman among them; ye never saw yin o' them yet the worse o' drink."

Elsewhere in the Para Handy stories Para points out that many of the Clyde steamers which didn't stretch to a full-scale German band had used just one instrumentalist:

I mind when the tippiest boats on the Clyde had chust wan decent fiddler or a poor man wantin' the eyesight wi' a concerteena.

The gaiety of a sail "doon the watter" was doubtless much assisted by the musical selections given by the band or the "wan decent fiddler". However a correspondent to the *Glasgow Herald* in 1888 felt moved to complain of:

. . . the torture of having to listen to the terrible musicians who apparently frequent our coast steamers.

Andrew McQueen writing in *Clyde River-Steamers of the last Fifty Years* in 1923 noted that by then:

The fiddler or harpist who found a place abaft the engine-house, and drew a haphazard remuneration from the caprice of the passengers, has given way to a uniformed band, whose collections are made on a business-like system.

This "business-like system" attracted the notice of the *Vital Spark's* engineer, Dan Macphail, who told Para Handy that if he wished the *Vital Spark* to go in for the passenger trade he would need to employ:

Yin o' thae bands that can feenish a'thegither even if they're playin' different tunes, or drap the piccolo oot every noo and then to go roond and lift the pennies.

The relationship of the Glaswegian, his river and the world served by his river's steamer services has always been a close one. Great interest has always been shown in the ships of the Clyde and the people of Glasgow quickly took to steamer sailing in a very big way, with holidays at the seaside resorts rapidly becoming the delight of all classes. City businessmen who could afford it took holiday homes in Arran or Argyllshire and packed the family off for the summer, sailing down to join them for the weekends and for a

PLEASURE CRUISES
TO
ARRAN
(not landing)

Daily, by Turbine Steamer

"KING EDWARD"
(OR OTHER STEAMER)

From GLASGOW Bridge Wharf (South Side) at 10 a.m.

Via Dunoon, Rothesay, Largs and Millport (Keppel).

	Steamer Outwards	Steamer Inwards	FARES FOR THE CRUISE	
	a.m.	p.m.	Saloon	F.-Saloon
GLASGOW Bridge Wharf (South Side)	10 0	8 15	5/-	4/-
GOVAN	10 10	8 5		
RENFREW	10 30	7 45	2/-	—
DUNOON	12 15p	5 55		
ROTHESAY arrive	1 0	—	1/6	—
ROTHESAY depart	1 15	5 20		
CRAIGMORE	1 20	5 0		
LARGS	2 0	4 30	1/-	
MILLPORT (Keppel)	2 10	4 10		

The Steamer will Cruise

On Mondays and Wednesdays	..	to BRODICK BAY
On Tuesdays and Thursdays	..	to LOCHRANZA
On Fridays	..	to CORRIE
On Saturdays		to GLEN SANNOX

Tickets are also issued from Glasgow, including meals, as under :

To Rothesay (Sal.), with Lunch and Plain Tea, **7/6**
Do.   do.   High Tea, **8/6**
Day's Sail (Sal.), with Lunch and Plain Tea, **9/-**
Do.   do.   High Tea, **10/-**

"QUEEN-EMPRESS" (or other Steamer) will sail on Saturdays.

For Sunday Services see page 9.

L.N.E.R. STEAMER NO3
SALOON
CRAIGENDORAN
AND
DUNOON or KIRN
Fare 1/1d. N
Available three months
from date of issue.
saloon
S3   For conditions
OR KIRN   see back
4526

DISCOVERING STRATHCLYDE

Sailing down the Clyde

Cal. S.P. Co. Ld. For   Cal. S.P. Co. Ld. For
conditions see Back.   conditions see Back.
Series (T)   Series (T)
SALOON   SALOON
SINGLE   SINGLE
BridgeWharf   BridgeWharf
GLASGOW Bridge Wharf &
ROTHESAY LARGS or MILLPORT
Rothesay &c.   Rothesay &c.
723   723
S   4/- P   FARE   4/- P   S

Strathclyde
Leisure & Recreation
Department

VICEROY HOUSE, INDIA STREET, GLASGOW, G2 4PF

fortnight's break. The poorer citizen had to be content with a few days at the Glasgow Fair in lodgings in Dunoon or Rothesay. A Glasgow poet of the Victorian era, Bass Kennedy, captured in *Doon the Watter at the Fair* the relationship between the workaday world of Glasgow and the Clyde and well illustrates the place that the river and the annual escape to the coast had in the affections of the people of the city. His speaker is a "Brigton weaver chiel" addressing his wife of thirty-five years:

> Ye min' yon July morn langsyne,
> A rosy morn like this,
> You pledged tae be for ever mine,
> An' sealed it wi' a kiss.
> On board the *Petrel*, near Dunoon,
> Ye yielded tae my prayer,
> An' aye sin' syne we've managed doon
> The watter at the Fair

> Sae haste ye, Nannie, come awa',
> An dinna langsome be,
> For thrangin' tae the Broomielaw,
> The focks gaun by wi' glee.
> A twalmonth's toil in Glesca toun
> Is lichtsome, I declare,
> Wi' twa-three days' diversion doon
> The watter at the Fair.

Still to be seen dominating the Broomielaw are the splendidly ornate premises built for the Clyde Navigation Trust (now Clydeport PLC). The original building in Robertson Street, designed by the prominent Glasgow architect J. J. Burnet, and dating from 1882-86 was extended in 1905-08. The lavish architectural decoration – Neptune, seahorses, busts of famous engineers – is a reflection of the confidence, prosperity and importance of the Port of Glasgow in the early part of this century and the building is rightly counted as one of the city's landmarks.

The Clyde Navigation Trust's origins go back to 1759 when the City Council was given power by Act of Parliament to "cleanse, scour, straighten and improve" the Clyde between Glasgow Bridge and Dumbuck Ford. Various other acts followed, increasing and extending the powers of the Trustees. The Trust was eventually composed of representatives of the City Council, the Trades' House, the Merchants' House, the Chamber of Commerce and shipowners.

The other old established public corporation with an active interest in the navigation of the Clyde was the Clyde Lighthouses Trust – a body governed jointly by the councils of Glasgow, Greenock and Port Glasgow. They established lighthouses on Cumbrae in 1793, at the Cloch near Gourock in 1797, these two lights being the work of Thomas Smith, and at Toward Point in Argyllshire in 1812, the work of Robert Stevenson, the founder of the famous dynasty of Scottish lighthouse engineers. The lighthouse on Cumbrae replaced a coal fired beacon which had been maintained on Little Cumbrae since 1757.

In 1966 the Clyde Port Authority was created by merging the Clyde Navigation Trust, the Greenock Harbour Trust and the Clyde Lighthouses Trust. The Clyde Port Authority in its turn was privatised by means of a management and employee buy-out in March 1992 which created Clydeport PLC which provides port services over a 450 square mile stretch of the river and firth of Clyde and has an annual turnover of £15.9 million. Clydeport, apart from its dock facilities in Glasgow and Greenock, operates a major deep water terminal at Hunterston on the Ayrshire coast with a mile long jetty which can accommodate the largest bulk carriers of up to 350,000 tons. Hunterston was designed for the efficient and rapid import and export of dry bulk cargoes such as ores, aggregates and coal. In fact the bulk of the traffic at Hunterston is made up of transshipments of coal for Northern Irish electricity generation although bulk exports of coal to continental destinations also form a significant part of its trade. Clydeport's second Ayrshire harbour is at Ardrossan, which enjoys a more varied pattern of business. Ardrossan is Clydeport's main centre for coastal traffic and is the base for both the Caledonian MacBrayne services to Arran and their summer service to the Isle of Man as well as for the roll-on roll-off trailer traffic to Northern Ireland. Ardrossan also imports chemical and other cargoes for local industry. The Clydeport area also includes the important British Petroleum oil terminal at Finnart on Loch Long which is linked by a cross-country pipeline to the British Petroleum refineries at Grangemouth on the Forth.

Downstream from the Navigation Trust Offices is an area of modern office development – Atlantic Quay. A riverside walkway connects the city centre with the down-river berths where the *Waverley* and *Tuxedo Princess* may be found in the winter months. The *Waverley* also lies here overnight in July and August between her busy programme of cruises and charters. There are however still traces of the old dockland to be found in this area, one example being the former Glasgow Seamen's Mission, built in 1926, at the corner of the Broomielaw and Brown Street. This has now, somewhat bizarrely, been converted into a discotheque. In James Watt Street can be seen a former Tobacco Warehouse, built in 1854 and reconstructed in 1911, reflecting just one of the exotic cargoes that once came into the heart of the city. This area also once held major whisky bonds, one of which, in Cheapside Street, was destroyed in a tragic fire in March 1960. Nineteen members of the Glasgow Fire Brigade and Salvage Corps lost their lives fighting this fire.

The River and Harbour area was once of sufficient importance to warrant possession of its own magistrate's court – the River Bailie Court. This building, though no longer used as such, and now rather sadly decayed, still stands in McAlpine Street – just a hundred yards from the Broomielaw. As might well be imagined, that somewhat uncertain skipper, Para Handy, found himself on one occasion up before the magistrate after the *Vital Spark* had collided with a French steamer. One of his crew was asked by the Bailie if he knew the rules of the road at sea and replied:

> It wass not my depairtment; I am only the cook and the winch; the Captain and Dougie attends to the fancy work. It iss likely the Captain would know aal about rules of the road.

Indeed the Captain should have known the rules because as early as 1816 the Clyde Trustees enacted regulations for "Steam-Boats and other Vessels, Plying on the Clyde". Among these were:

> III That when Steam-Boats attempt to pass each other from astern, the boat which sails slowest shall give way to the larboard, (left hand side) for the faster sailing boat to pass, when the latter comes within thirty yards of the former, under penalty of £5 for each offence, besides damages.
> IV That when the said boats sailing in opposite directions, meet, each shall keep to the larboard side, so as to afford all possible facility to each other in passing, under the like penalty of £5 for each offence, besides damages.

The original steamer services on the Clyde had, of course, been "all the way sailings". However in the late nineteenth century the foul condition of the river, which received the untreated sewage of the city until the opening of a treatment plant at Dalmarnock in 1894, made such sailings understandably much less popular and the preferred route was a railway journey to Craigendoran, Greenock or Gourock and a steamer connection from there on to the final destination. In the 1930s when the Williamson steamer *Queen Mary* was introduced on the company's services from Bridge Wharf (South Side) it was remarked that no new ship of her quality had been provided for the all the way sailing for many years. J. J. Bell, writing in the 1930s, noted that there had been a time:

> . . . when passengers regarded with disfavour those narrow murky waters, and tried not to breathe, but that was before Glasgow had conquered her sewage problem, and to-day the tide, though far from crystalline, ebbs and flows without offence.

Berths near James Watt Street were used by Burns & Laird Line Ltd. for their Irish sailings. This old established company, whose origins can be traced back to 1825, ran services to Londonderry, Belfast, Dublin and Sligo. The Burns boats had traditionally used animal names – *Tiger, Adder, Vulture* etc. After the merger of G. & J, Burns and Laird Line Ltd, in 1922 the company's ships were , in 1929, renamed to incorporate the word "Laird": thus the *Vulture* became *Lairdsrock*.

In the early part of this century these Irish services were especially busy at the time of the Glasgow Fair. Glasgow had attracted a large number of Irish immigrants over the years – especially from Donegal and other northern areas and the Fair was

Newspaper advert from 1962.

GLASGOW and ARDROSSAN TO BELFAST
GLASGOW TO DUBLIN
GLASGOW TO LONDONDERRY

Direct Services For this year's holiday in IRELAND

PASSENGERS, MOTOR CARS

FULL INFORMATION FROM

BURNS & LAIRD LINES LTD.
56 Robertson Street Glasgow C.2 Telephone CENtral 6301
—or your local Travel Agent

Royal Scotsman (1936) prior to maiden voyage.

Lairdsglen (1954) with *Ferry No. 2* and dredger *Craigiehall* (1903).

a popular time for them to visit friends and family back home in Ireland. Erchie McPherson, Neil Munro's observant beadle noted this phenomenon, as he noted so much else of the city's life:

> I went doon to the Broomielaw on Setturday to see Jinnet aff, and the croods on the Irish and Hielan' boats was that awfu', the men at the steerage end hadna room to pu' oot their pocket-hankies if they needed them. It's lucky they could dae withoot. When the butter-and-egg boats for Belfast and 'Derry left the quay, the pursers had a' to have on twa watches – at least they had the twa watch-chains, ane on each side, for fear the steamer wad capsize.

The great business, other than passengers, of Burns & Laird, was the importation of agricultural produce from Ireland to Scotland – hence Erchie's reference to "butter-and-egg boats". One of Glasgow's most famous sons, Thomas Lipton, laid the foundation of his immense fortune by importing butter, cheese and bacon directly from Ireland and doubtless the Burns & Laird boats carried many a load for Lipton's shops. The extent of this trade is suggested by the fact that 14,810 tons of eggs were imported into Glasgow docks in 1887 – most of this presumably coming from Ireland. We tend not to think of eggs in tons and one hesitates to calculate the actual number of eggs involved – suffice it to say that it would make a pretty substantial omelette!

The Glasgow to Belfast overnight service was covered by two ships; until 1936 *Lairdscastle* and *Lairdsburn*, and thereafter *Royal Scotsman* and *Royal Ulsterman*. From Monday to Saturday inclusive, the ships would leave each port at 9 p.m. and return the following evening. Dublin and Londonderry each had their own service which left Glasgow at 6.30 p.m., three times weekly. Latterly *Lairdshill* sailed to Dublin and *Lairdsloch* to 'Derry. *Irish Coast*, likewise built by Harland and Wolff, Belfast, would frequently operate to Dublin. When, in 1969, the car ferry *Lion* came into service on the Ardrossan to Belfast service the remaining cattle and passenger services from the Broomielaw ceased and a long-standing Glasgow tradition was ended.

The Coast Line, running cargo service to Liverpool with vessels such as the *Ayrshire Coast* and *Cumberland Coast,* also operated from this area. Their vessels displayed a black funnel with a white chevron.

Near the Irish boat's berth was the base for the West coast cargo services operated by McCallum Orme & Co. Like many of the Clyde ship owners this company was formed out of a complex series of mergers and take-overs and could trace its origins back to the mid nineteenth century. McCallum Orme's business was

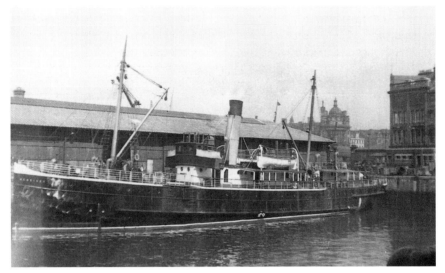

Hebrides (1898) in Kingston Dock.

Dunara Castle (1875)

absorbed by MacBraynes in 1947. Their best known ships engaged in the West Highland service in the inter-war period were the *Hebrides* and *Dunara Castle*. The latter was particularly associated with sailings to St Kilda and indeed took part in the final evacuation of these remote islands in August 1930. *Hebrides* had taken off some of the islanders' sheep in July but *Dunara Castle* completed the evacuation of livestock and carried away from the island post office what was to be, for many years, the last batch of mail to bear the coveted St Kilda post mark.

Dunara Castle, incidentally, had a remarkable record of service, being built by Blackwood and Gordon at Port Glasgow in 1875 and continued its regular round of the Hebrides until it was withdrawn in 1948, aged 73. Not indeed that this was the Clyde's record for endurance – *Glencoe*, built as the *Mary Jane* by Tod and MacGregor at Meadowside in 1846 was still running Messrs MacBrayne's mail service to Portree in 1931 in her 85th year – the concept of built-in obsolescence clearly was not known to the Clyde's ship-builders or shipowners! The current record for longevity in active service must rest with the *Sir Walter Scott*, built in 1900 by Denny at Dumbarton and still cruising on Loch Katrine – although this record has, admittedly, been achieved in the much less harsh environment of an inland fresh water loch.

Indeed many Clyde steamers, when their service on the river was over, were transferred to less demanding areas. Neil Munro describes this process:

> Clyde ships, second-hand, grown obsolete for Glasgow passengers, go, at the end, to less fastidious quarters, so that "crocks" from the Clyde have glorified the lower Thames and provided a standard of elegance for the traveller to Clacton and Southend; and elsewhere in English waters the Scotsman often comes upon old friends of the "Fair" holidays working under aliases. Such good stuff are those old Clyde passenger steamers that they seem immortal, and their owners buff out the natal dates on their bells and engine brasses, ashamed perhaps, to be found demanding the labour of youth from such veterans.

Not for nothing did Munro describe the Clyde as "the Scottish ship shop".

Bridge Wharf

This was originally known as Clyde Place Quay but was reconstructed as Bridge Wharf in the late 1920s. The 1929 Clyde Navigation Trust buildings with the clock tower can still be seen immediately downstream from King George V Bridge and the condition of the quayside, although shabby and run-down does, unlike many other parts of Glasgow's river, still suggest something of the Clydeside scene in its hey-day. Steamer services from Bridge Wharf started on the King's Birthday Holiday – Monday May 20th 1929, with the *Iona* sailing at 7.11 a.m. for Ardrishaig and ceased in 1969 when on Sunday 15th September the *Caledonia* carried out the final sailing. Some nautical flavour is still retained by the presence of a yacht agent and the Renfrew Ferry night club at the downstream end of the wharf, although the lack of dredging on this stretch of the river means that the Renfrew Ferry can be left stranded high and dry at low water.

The *Waverley* (1947) leaving Bridge Wharf, with the *Queen Mary II* backing up to berth. A Clyde trust dredger is moored at the quay.

King Edward (1901) at Bridge Wharf 1931.

Eagle III (1910) leaving the Bridge Wharf (south side) in the early 1930's.

Caledonia (1934) at Bridge Wharf, 1960.

Windmillcroft Quay

This quay was formerly the base for the Bristol Channel services operated by the ships of William Sloan & Company. This company's practice was to name their vessels after rivers and so the *Annan, Beauly, Brora, Findhorn, Orchy* and *Severn* could be seen here. The company was absorbed into Coast Lines Ltd. in 1958. Their regular Bristol service ceased in 1968.

Beauly (1924) passing Clydebank.

Kingston Dock

Behind Windmillcroft Quay was the Kingston Dock. This was built in 1867 to house the larger sailing vessels and provided 5½ acres of water and 823 yards of quay in a lockless basin with a steam-operated swing bridge over the entrance. Among the companies to use this dock were MacBrayne and McCallum Orme & Company. Other regular visitors were vessels importing china-clay from Cornwall – a reminder that the Glasgow area once had a substantial pottery industry. Kingston Dock was also used by the Imperial Chemical Industries vessels from Fleetwood, with their appropriate names such as *Barium, Calcium, Helium* and *Sodium.*

Although by the early years of the twentieth century the sailing ship was certainly very much in decline there remained a surprisingly large amount of cargo traffic being carried by sail. For example in 1912/13 there were 39,000 recorded movements of coastal sailing ships into UK ports, compared to 129,000 movements of steamships, and the steamer had only probably achieved its leading position in coastal trade movements as late as the 1890s. Kingston Dock was still the favoured location for most of the sailing ships trading into the Port of Glasgow. When, on

18th June 1914, a major fire destroyed most of Kingston Dock there were five wooden schooners among the other vessels in harbour. One schooner managed to escape but the other four were destroyed. Their burnt out hulks were towed down to Newshot Isle where their remains are still to be seen. Damage to the Dock was estimated at £160,000, and subsequent investigations revealed that the cause of the fire had been workmen, engaged on improvements, drilling in creosote soaked piles along the quay wall. These quickly caught fire and a major blaze ensued. Some of the redundant Clutha ferries were pressed into service as fire tenders and one valuable lesson learned from

Queen's Dock and Stobcross Quay.
Photo: Hunting Aerofilms Ltd.

Ardyne (1928) in Kingston Dock.

the incident was the need for a proper fire float for the river. The Dock was rebuilt after the fire and continued in operation until 1966 when it had to be closed to allow work to start on the construction of the Kingston Bridge. Like many riverfront areas the Windmillcroft and the Kingston Dock sites have now been redeveloped for housing.

The MacBrayne's cargo boats which had been using Kingston Dock up until its closure transferred a few hundred yards down river and continued their cargo service to the West Highlands and the islands until 1976. The part that MacBrayne's services traditionally played in the life of the West Highlands is suggested by the not entirely affectionate verse which runs:

The earth unto the Lord belongs and all that it contains
Except, of course the Western Isles and these are all MacBrayne's.

The novelist Neil Munro, himself an Inveraray man and thus well able to appreciate the part that MacBrayne's vessels played in the life of the West Highlands, its economy and culture, wrote in the early years of this century:

Along the western sea-board, from Tarbert, Loch Fyne, to Lochinver, and throughout the Inner and Outer Isles from Port Ellen in Islay to Stornoway in the Lews, generations of young Highlanders have grown up with the idea that their very existence was more or less dependent on MacBrayne. But for

> MacBrayne, most of them would never have seen bananas or the white loaf of the lowlands; might still be burning coalfish oil in crusies, and getting no more than sixpence a dozen for their eggs.

Munro goes on to confess :

> I was sixteen years old before I discovered that all the steamers in the world had not red funnels with black tops. Up till then I was of the impression that the same colour was officially used for steamboats, letter-boxes, soldier's coats, penny stamps, and Union Jacks.

This reference to the distinctive livery of MacBrayne's may remind ship spotters that exactly the same funnel colours have traditionally been used by the Cunard Line. This is no accident and the connection comes through the work of the Clyde shipbuilder and engineer Robert Napier. Napier also had shipowning interests and his steamers ran in red and black funnel colours – Napier's fleet was one of the origins of the MacBrayne company which adopted these colours. Napier, as we shall see later, built the first four ships for Samuel Cunard and was a substantial shareholder in the Cunard Company – the splendidly named British and American Royal Mail Steam Packet Company – and he had the funnels of the first Cunarders painted in his own house colours.

R Kingston Bridge

The most recent and most spectacular of the city's road bridges was completed in 1970 as part of the city's extensive programme of road building. The bridge offers a 60 foot clearance over the river – a height dictated by the need to allow dredgers to operate upriver as far as King George V Bridge. In anticipation of the bridge being built all four of the then remaining Clyde cruise steamers – *Caledonia, Waverley, Queen Mary II* and *Duchess of Hamilton* had their masts reduced in height during the winter refits of 1968-69 to allow them to come up-river to use Bridge Wharf. However Bridge Wharf did not feature in the 1970 sailing lists so this mast reduction proved to be a fruitless exercise which only succeeded in spoiling the ships' appearance.

S Springfield Quay

This is the first of a series of quays – Springfield, General Terminus and Mavisbank Quays which stretched downriver between the modern Kingston Bridge and Prince's Dock. They fell into decline in the late 1950s and saw little traffic after the mid 1960s.

Clyde Shipping Company Vessel *Rathlin* (1936), Springfield Quay 1937.

Findhorn (1903) at General Terminus buoys.

Springfield Quay was used by the ships of the Clyde Shipping Company, the oldest continuing owner of steamships in the world. The company's services concentrated on sailings to London but they also served ports such as Belfast, Waterford, Limerick and Cork as well as English destinations which included Liverpool, Southampton and Dover. Their ships were named after lighthouses and ships such as *Toward, Eddystone, Skerryvore* and *Fastnet* could be seen berthed here. These cargo and passenger services offered excellent value for money with a 1930s sailing,

Tuesday to Sunday, Glasgow to Dublin, Waterford and Cork, and back, being offered for a modest fare of £3, exclusive of meals.

General Terminus Quay had been built in 1849 for coal traffic, which included the export of coal overseas and domestic coal movements by coasters and puffers to Scottish and Irish ports. Coal was in fact the largest export, by volume, from the Port of Glasgow – in 1887 831,356 tons were shipped out. The second largest bulk cargo was pig iron – with 191,120 tons being exported in 1887.

In this century, with the increasing use of oil fuels in shipping and in industry, the coal trade declined. General Terminus Quay increasingly became used for the importation of iron ore for the Lanarkshire steel industry. New berths with three cranes, which became riverside landmarks, were completed in 1957. The first ship to discharge at this new facility was the Swedish ship *Rautus* which unloaded 10,300 tons of iron ore on 7th January 1958. The rebuilt Quay had been provided at a cost of nearly £2 million by the leading Scottish steelmaking company, Colvilles Ltd., in association with the Clyde Navigation Trust. Colvilles' complex of steel works in Lanarkshire required, at this period, to import two million tons of iron ore per annum. This iron ore had formerly come into Rothesay Dock, lower down the Clyde, but the new facility at General Terminus Quay allowed a typical ship-load of over 15,000 tons to be discharged in two days rather than the seven days which would have been needed at the older dock. As the years went on, however, the ever increasing size of ore-carriers resulted in the development of a deep water ore terminal at Hunterston on the Ayrshire coast. Sadly the iron industry has now declined and ore carriers ceased to call at General Terminus Quay which gradually fell into disuse and the three giant unloaders were blown up.

In the middle of the river, opposite General Terminus Quay, were to be found a number of moorings – the General Terminus Buoys. Between the wars these were commonly used for laid up coasters and the cargo-carrying *Sanda* of the Clyde Shipping Company was to be seen laid up here in the summer months to be brought into winter service when there was little demand for passenger accommodation on her routes. Sloan's *Annan* was laid up here in the 1930s until she was refitted in 1937 as a car transporter, accommodating the grand total of seven motor vehicles! She was used to transport new cars from the Oxford works of Morris Motors – the cars were loaded on to *Annan* at one of the Bristol Channel ports and brought to the Clyde for distribution throughout the West of Scotland.

N Anderston Quay

Spanned by the Kingston Bridge is Anderston Quay whose present day shipping interest is confined to the night-club ship *Tuxedo Princess*. She was built in 1961 by William Denny & Brothers of Dumbarton as *Caledonian Princess*, a car ferry for the Stranraer-Larne service of British Railways subsidiary Caledonian Steam Packet Company (Irish Services) Ltd.

Anderston Quay lies in what was once the totally separate Burgh of Anderston. This was created as a planned village in 1725, created a burgh in 1824 and annexed by Glasgow in 1846. Many of the other riverside areas of what is now Glasgow were once fiercely independent burghs; Gorbals was incorporated into the city in the same year as Anderston, while Govan and Partick were only absorbed into Glasgow, against considerable local opposition, in 1912.

N Lancefield Quay

Downriver from Anderston Quay we come to Lancefield Quay, now used as the base for the *Waverley*, the last of the Clyde's long line of paddle steamers. The *Waverley* has been based here from 1975-1977 and again from 1983 to the present and her workshops and offices are also located here. Between 1978 and 1982 *Waverley* sailed from Stobcross Quay. The booking office used by the *Waverley* was formerly used by both MacBrayne and by Burns Laird.

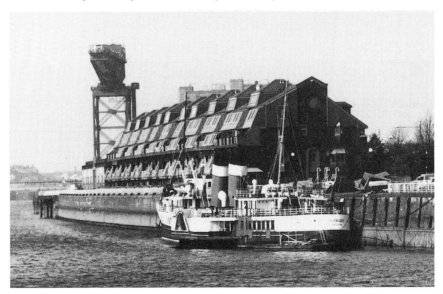

Waverley at her winter berth, Stobcross Crane is in the background., 1995.

The area behind Lancefield Quay was once the hub of Glasgow's early marine engineering world. Lancefield Works were established here by David Napier in 1821. Later, in 1836, the works passed into the ownership of David Napier's cousin Robert Napier and many engines for early steamers were built here before Robert built a new iron shipbuilding yard at Govan. Earlier, David had owned the Vulcan Foundry in Washington Street (just upstream from the Kingston Bridge). The Lancefield Works produced the engines for the first four ships for the Cunard Line in 1840.

The remarkable development of the harbour area in the last century is shown by the statistics of the total length of quay at various dates. In 1800 the city had only 382 yards of quay at the Broomielaw. By 1840 quays on the North and South bank totalled 1,973 yards, by 1860 this had more than doubled to 4,376 yards and by 1880 6,279 yards were available. This figure is simply the extent of the river front quayage and excludes the extensive wharfage available in the various docks.

↑N Finnieston Quay

There has always been pressure on the river crossings in Glasgow and during the late 1920's and 1930's there was a long-running campaign to build a bridge at Finnieston. Finnieston had been the site of a passenger and vehicular ferry, which, in anticipation of the

Vehicular Ferryboat No.3 (1913), *Ferry No. 6* is at the steps with the diving bell at the quayside.

Ferry No.10 (1934) at General Terminus in 1972.

bridge's construction, was moved a little upstream to Elliot Street at Lancefield Quay. The Finnieston Tunnel was built in 1890-96 at the height of the age of horse transport. The two domed rotundas on the North and South Banks which once gave access to this tunnel, or rather complex of tunnels, are still to be seen. As built there was a North-bound and a South-bound tunnel for horse traffic and a two-way pedestrian tunnel. The tunnels also carried a water main across the Clyde. Hydraulically powered vehicle lifts in the rotundas took the wheeled traffic down to the tunnel level – while stairs provided access for pedestrians. Vehicular traffic through the tunnel ceased in 1943 and the lift machinery was removed. Pedestrian access was re-instated in 1947 and continued until 1980. The North Rotunda is now a restaurant.

The Finnieston to Plantation passenger ferry – ferry number 10 – was preserved when it came out of service in the 1970s and is now based at Kirkintilloch on the Forth & Clyde Canal as the floating restaurant barge *Caledonian*. Another Clyde passenger ferry, this time ferry number 8 from the Kelvinhaugh crossing, is also retained on the Canal as the Forth & Clyde Canal Society's excursion boat *Ferry Queen*.

Ŝ Stobcross Quay

This quay ran between Finnieston Quay and the entrance to Queen's Dock. It once was widely used by various shipping lines and here in particular, at the upper end, could be seen the South American cargo ships. Down river was the berth for the Anchor Line's Indian service operated by their ships such as *Circassia*, *Massilia* and *Scindia*. Stobcross Quay was also often brought into use by nearby shipbuilders for fitting out new vessels.

The distinctive feature of Stobcross Quay today is the large, and recently refurbished crane. This 175 ton crane was erected by the Clyde Navigation Trust in 1931 specifically for loading heavy railway locomotives. If shipbuilding was Glasgow and the West of Scotland's great heavy engineering industry, undoubtedly the runner up was the construction of railway locomotives. Glasgow housed the engine works of the Caledonian Railway and Kilmarnock was the home of Andrew Barclay, Sons & Company, a prominent company of locomotive engineers. However the largest firm in this industry was the North British Locomotive Company.

Looking down-river from the city, showing King George V bridge, Broomielaw (right) leading to Stobcross Quay and Queen's Dock (now the S.E.C.C.) with Kingston Dock (left) and Bridge Wharf.
Photo: Hunting Aerofilms Ltd.

Stobcross Quay and the Finnieston Crane.
Photo: Mitchell Library, Glasgow.

This undertaking had been formed in 1903 by the merger of three long established firms of Glasgow locomotive builders. North British Locomotive in the 1950s employed over 5,000 employees at their works in the North of Glasgow and exported 90% of their output. The sight of newly built steam and diesel locomotives being moved through the city on their low-loaders was a familiar and stirring spectacle. In the early years of the century, before the development of sufficiently powerful lorries, these heavy loads were drawn down to the Docks by steam road locomotives. The North British Locomotive Company went into liquidation in 1962.

The Stobcross Crane was also used to engine several ships built in Clyde yards which lacked fitting-out berths. Most of these vessels were supplied with engines by the nearby firm of David Rowan and Company.In recent years this landmark of the Glasgow waterfront was used to display the Scottish sculptor George Wylie's model of the *Queen Mary* and his tribute to the Glasgow railway engineering tradition – "The Straw Locomotive". Crane no. 7 was also used for the re-boilering of the *Waverley* in the winter of 1980/81 and retains a strategic function as a potential means of loading heavy armaments into naval vessels.

Ñ Queen's Dock

Where the Scottish Exhibition and Conference Centre and the Moat House Hotel now stand was once the site of Queen's Dock . Of this massive complex constructed between 1872 and 1880 the only significant remaining trace is the former Hydraulic Pumping Station which was converted to a restaurant in 1988. Otherwise the Dock was closed in 1969 with the dredger *Blythswood* dumping loads of silt to fill in the basins. The site lay derelict until the Conference Centre was completed in 1987.

In its earlier days Queen's Dock was one of the most important of the Glasgow docks. It had a central quay with a basin lying to either side. In the Northern basin could be seen ships of the Clan Line and P. Henderson & Co., commonly known as Paddy Henderson ships. The latter company specialised in the trade between Britain and Burma and the company's ships had names appropriate to that trade – *Chindwin, Burma, Amarapoora* etc. Sailing through the Mediterranean and the Suez Canal they offered a pleasant and popular passenger service to the Far East and intermediate destinations. During the 1930s, a return trip from Glasgow to Palma, Majorca was offered using outward bound Paddy Henderson vessels and returning overland via France. Both the Clan Line and Paddy Henderson employed Indian deck crews – the Lascar seamen who Neil Munro described as:

. . . shivering in thin dongarees

---

and indeed the contrast between their Indian homes and their cold Glasgow port of call must have been very striking. East Indian seamen were increasingly used from the end of the nineteenth century by many of the major shipping lines trading between Britain and the Indian sub-continent. Among the other companies who employed Lascars as deck, engineering and catering hands were P & O, British India, Bibby, Brocklebank, Clan, City and Anchor Lines. Most of these Asian seafarers were from India but the Henderson line was, understandably, increasingly to use Burmese personnel.

At the top of the North basin and lying at right angles to the main dock was the berth of Glen & Company who operated timber ships to Gothenburg in Sweden. These vessels, the *Orsa, Shuna, Varna* or *Winga*, always came in loaded with timber stacked high on their well-decks. Here also could be found ships of the Currie Line, the Leith Hull and Hamburg Steam Packet Company, which served Hamburg and Bremen. A round trip to the Baltic in one of their vessels, such as the *Rhineland, Rutland* or *Shetland* cost

Hays puffers occupy a corner of Queen's Dock, 1958

The *Slav* and *Turk* in Queen's Dock 1958

£12 in the 1930s. Nearer to the entrance of the dock was a coaling berth. Wagon loads of coal came to the dock, and were lifted by a crane and tipped into the bunkers of the waiting ships.

At the entrance to the South side basin could be seen *Procris, Smerdis, Arethusa* and *Busiris*, the coasters of J. & P. Hutchison – a company which later merged with Moss Line of Liverpool to form the Moss Hutchison Line. Their ships served the ports of Northern France, Spain and Portugal.

The South side of the central quay was used exclusively by the ships of the Ellerman Group – City Line, Hall Line, Ellerman Line and Bucknall Line. The City Line had been originally a Glasgow owned company but with its incorporation into the Ellerman Group the City Line identity was gradually lost and the distinctive dark hull with the ship's name standing out in individually applied letters became a less and less familiar sight. The Bucknall Line ships were easily identifiable with their black funnels, circled at the top with a row of white diamond shapes – known to the trade as "Bucknall's Teeth". In the off season for Indian passenger trade two of the City Line's large passenger liners *City of Nagpur* and *City of Paris* were often laid up here. With all this activity there is little wonder that a plan showing the ships in port used to be displayed on the signal tower at the Dock entrance.

The turret deck Clan liner – *Clan Buchanan* in the late 1890's. The odd-looking turret deck design was used to minimise a vessel's deck surface area as dues charged in the Suez Canal at this time were assessed on this basis. As late as the 1920's, ships of this type were to be seen at Clan Line's berths in Queen's Dock.

In *Glasgow in 1901* by James Hamilton Muir we get a colourful and evocative description of the port of Glasgow and its trade at, perhaps, its peak.

If you compare Glasgow with other large ports, perhaps its most distinguishing feature is the comprehensive nature of its trading. The liner *de luxe*, as Liverpool people understand her in the *Oceanic* or the *Campania* or the *St. Louis*, is not to be seen on the narrow Clyde; and the Cardiff man, accustomed to his miles of coal traders, will find disappointment here; still, if you were to spend a diligent morning in the docks, you will find few types of the British mercantile marine amissing. The Transatlantic passenger steamers of the Allan and Anchor firms, the strange East-Coastish lines of the Donaldson carriers ("lines like a hat-box," as an old skipper had it), the queer-shaped turret ships of the Clan Company, which look as though they had swallowed much more cargo than they could digest, the big bright-funnelled South American traders, bristling with derricks and samson-posts; the China Mutual steamers, with their names in the script of Far Cathay on their bows; the Loch Line sailing ships, which clip Australian records every season as keen as any "greyhound of the Atlantic"; the four-masted Frenchman from New Caledonia, the teak-carrier from Rangoon, the auxiliary screw laden with seal oil and skins from Harbour Grace, the nitrate barque from Chili, the City steamers from India and the Persian Gulf – you can find them all. Then there are the squadrons of tramps which thrash from Bilbao to the Clyde with ore and back again with coal; the Italian fruit boats, the stout cross-channel packets, the Highland steamers, and topsail schooners which congregate in the Kingston Dock.

At the time the above extract was written Glasgow was the third British port, after London and Liverpool, in terms of net registered shipping. Although by the turn of the century the great age of sail could be seen to be in decline there were still four major Glasgow-based sailing ship companies – the Shire Line with 27 ships, Loch Line with 16 ships, Port Line with 10 and County Line with 9. Among the city's steamship lines the Clan Line with 41 vessels, the Anchor Line with 32, Allan Line with 32, Maclay & McIntyre with 47 and Burrell and Son with 27 ships were perhaps pre-eminent. The owner of Burrell & Sons, William Burrell, was of course to win fame outwith the shipping world for his role as an art collector. His munificent gift to his native city of Glasgow of his enormous collection of art and antiquities is now housed in a specially designed gallery at Pollok, opened in 1983.

The Southern entrance to Queen's Dock accommodated a ferry stance used for triangular service between Queen's Dock, Yorkhill, and Highland Lane in Govan – this service ceased during the 1920s.

Queen's Dock, like many other areas of Glasgow's docks and harbour, was constructed on what proved to be very difficult ground. Excavations revealed that the foundations would be mostly located on water-bearing gravel and sand with some areas of mud. The extensive and massive construction required could only be achieved by sinking groups of concrete cylinders to form the foundations for the docks.

Plantation & Mavisbank Quays

These quays stretched downriver from General Terminus Quay and were particularly used by refrigerated vessels from the Port Line and the New Zealand Shipping Company, T. & J. Harrison and the Federal Steam Navigation Company. In the late 1970s and early 80s Plantation Quay often found itself being called into service as berths for laying-up unwanted vessels.

MacBrayne paddlers *Chevalier* (1866) and *Mountaineer* (1852) at Mavisbank Quay.   C. 1871

Opposite: Riverside berth at Plantation Quay looking over to Stobcross Quay at entrance to Queen's Dock.
Photo: Mitchell Library, Glasgow.

Mavisbank Quay was the point of departure for the cargo service to Antwerp and Ghent operated by the British and Continental Steamship Company of Liverpool. This company's custom was to name their ships after birds and the white funnels of the *Avocet, Bittern, Cormorant* and their sister-ships were to be spotted, appropriately enough, at this Quay named after the blackbird – or mavis.

In an earlier period Mavisbank Quay had been the first Glasgow premises of the shipbuilders Tod & MacGregor and one of the early steamers built by them at Mavisbank in 1843, the *Emperor*, created a major scandal on the river, and indeed throughout Scotland, in 1853. In July of that year the papers carried an advertisement for Sunday sailings on the *Emperor* from the Broomielaw. This was the first open breach of the Sabbath by pleasure sailings and caused a storm of protest. Three hundred and fifty people bought tickets for the first sailing, even larger crowds turned out to witness the spectacle, while the Presbytery of Glasgow condemned:

> . . . an enterprise which daringly violates the Law of God, which openly insults the Lord of the Sabbath day and which audaciously outrages the feelings of the whole Christian community.

Quite how outraged the Christian community was is revealed by the extraordinary events which took place when the *Emperor* tried to call at Garelochhead pier on 21st August 1853. The pier owner, who was the local landlord and also, incidentally, the Lord Lieutenant of the County of Dunbarton, Sir James Colquhoun of Luss, called out his estate workers and the police force and barricaded the village pier. The *Emperor's* skipper insisted on his right to land and a pitched battle broke out, to the shock and scandal of the villagers coming back from the church. In subsequent weeks the Minister of the nearby village of Rhu led his parishioners to Rhu pier in an attempt to prevent *Emperor* berthing at that landing place.

The *Emperor* case was fought, slightly more sedately, through the courts, ending up with a verdict of the Court of Session which confirmed Sir James's right to close his piers on Sundays. Sunday sailings continued, using public as opposed to private piers, and attracted a rather bad reputation – chiefly because the river steamers were exempted from licensing regulations and the Sunday boats became largely an excuse for drinking excursions. In the 1880s legislation was introduced prohibiting the sale of drink on Sunday day-trip sailings.

℞ Bell's Bridge

The most recent of the Clyde crossings, this pedestrian bridge was designed by engineers Crouch and Hogg in 1988 for the Scottish Development Agency to link the Scottish Exhibition and Conference Centre on the old Queen's Dock site with the Garden Festival site (see below) which was being developed on the area once occupied by Prince's Dock. The bridge pivots on one of its piers to allow the passage of ships, and this facility is now chiefly used to accommodate the twice daily passages of the *Waverley* during her summer sailings on the Clyde on Fridays, Saturdays and Sundays.

℞ Prince's Dock

This extensive dock complex was built behind the line of Plantation Quay between 1893 and 1897 and was originally to be called Cessnock Dock. The increasing size of ships using the port of Glasgow was reflected in the unbridged entrance to the dock and the extensive manoeuvring area – the canting basin – which lay in

Prince's Dock, 1929. This became the site of the Glasgow Garden Festival in 1988. Photo: Hunting Aerofilms Ltd.

front of the three unloading basins. Each of these basins was lined with two storey brick and steel built sheds for the accommodation of goods in transit. The dock was equipped with hydraulically powered cranes and one of the hydraulic pumping stations still survives at the South-East corner of the site facing Govan Road. This handsome and highly decorated building, which features relief panels representing the Four Winds, was built in 1894 and designed by Burnet, Son & Campbell. Another accumulator tower, of 1911-12, stands opposite Govan Town Hall at the western extremity of the dock area. Otherwise nothing other than the canting basin remains of this splendid dock. It was infilled and landscaped to form the site for the Glasgow Garden Festival of 1988 and was thereafter scheduled to be developed for housing, however plans now exist for the creation of a £40 million project incorporating a Scottish National Science Centre at Pacific Quay. The Science Centre, designed to attract 600,000 visitors per year and to promote the popular understanding of science, would be complemented by an Imax 3-D film theatre, other leisure and retailing developments as well as a business park providing quality low rise accommodation. The most striking feature of the site is planned to be a 100 metre high Millenium Tower, whose observation platform will offer breathtaking views over the city.

Among the lines using the Prince's Dock in the inter-war period was the Donaldson Line. This company ran scheduled services between the Clyde and Montreal and Quebec using ships such as the *Letitia* and *Athenia*. The *Athenia*, built in 1922 at Fairfield yard was outward bound from the Clyde when she was torpedoed and sunk without warning off the Irish coast on 3rd September 1939. This sinking, by the German submarine U30, resulted in the loss of 112 lives and the *Athenia* became the first merchant ship casualty of the Second World War.

The Donaldson Line also served the Canadian Atlantic ports, and via the Panama Canal, the Canadian Pacific Coast ports such as Vancouver. The line's South American subsidiary traded with five ships to Montevideo and Buenos Ayres.

The Canadian Pacific Railway's ships, such as the *Metagama*, also used this dock for their emigrant traffic up to 1930. It is perhaps difficult now to appreciate the scale of emigration from Britain in the nineteenth century and the first half of the twentieth century or the importance that the emigrant trade had for British shipping. Many shipping lines were deeply dependent on this traffic for their livelihood and regular sailings were carried out to the main migrant centres of the United States, Canada, Australia and

Metagama (1915) in Prince's Dock following a collision with the *Baron Vernon* in 1923.

New Zealand. It has been estimated that over 2.3 million Scots emigrated between 1825 and 1938 – the highest percentage emigration rate of any European country. Much of this traffic went from the Clyde and, it should be remembered, the Clyde also served as a convenient point of departure for many emigrants from outwith Scotland.

Robert Louis Stevenson sailed to America in 1879 from the Broomielaw on board the steamer *Devonia*. He described his experiences in *The Amateur Emigrant* – and gives us an impression of the composition of his fellow passengers, the real emigrants:

"There were Scots and Irish in plenty, a few English, a few Americans, a good handful of Scandinavians, a German or two, and one Russian. . . "

The conditions on the emigrant ships was often far from good. Stevenson describes the steerage accommodation on the *Devonia*, the area used by the poorest migrants:

Steerage No. 1 is shaped like an isosceles triangle, the sides opposite the equal angles bulging out with the contours of the ship. It is lined with eight pens of sixteen bunks apiece, four bunks below and four above on either side. . . When the pen was fully occupied, with sixteen live human animals, more or less unwashed, lying immersed together in the same close air all night, and their litter of meat, dirty dishes and rank bedding being tumbled all day together in foul disorder, the merest possibilities of health or cleanliness were absent. If it was impossible to clean the steerage, it was no less impossible to clean the steerage passenger. All ablution below was rigorously forbidden. A man might give his hands a scour at the pump beside the galley, but that was exactly all.

Devonia (1877), off Greenock. Anchor Liner, accommodation for 1100 passengers in 3 classes. It's maiden voyage was from Glasgow to New York.

The marked downturn in the emigrant trade in the mid-twentieth century was to be a major element in the decline of the Clyde as both a shipbuilding river and a port. A graphic and poetic description of the bustle of life and activity in Glasgow's docks and harbours in the first years of the twentieth century is given by Neil Munro in his *"The Clyde – River and Firth"*:

Nor even then can one rightly comprehend the harbour who has not brooded beside sheer-leg and crane-jib that are mightily moving enormous weights as if they had been toys; swallowed the coal-dust of the docks; dodged traction engines, eaten Irish stew for breakfast in the Sailors' Homes, watched Geordie Geddes trawl for corpses, sat in the fo'c'sles of "tramps", stood in a fog by the pilot on the bridge, heard the sorrows of a Shore

Opposite: *The Empress of Canada* (1922), at Prince's Dock, 1929.

> Superintendent and the loyal lies of witnesses in a Board of Trade
> examination, who feel bound to "stick by the owners" and swear
> their engines backed ten minutes before the accident; or sat on
> a cask in the Prince's Dock on peaceful Sabbath mornings when
> the shipping seemed asleep, or an unseen concertina played some
> sailor's jig for canticle.

Smaller Scottish companies based on Prince's Dock included John
Bruce & Company and Whimster & Company who ran services
between Glasgow and the Central Mediterranean. As late as the
mid 1960s Whimster's ships, by then owned by Constantine of
Middlesborough, were still offering four or five passenger berths on
their Mediterranean sailings and a five-week round cruise could be
had for about £130.

In the early summer of each year between the wars the "Grain
Race" from Australia would take place with the last of the big
sailing ships carrying the new season's crop back to Europe.
Usually two of these ships would end up in Prince's Dock, berthing
in the South-eastern corner. The arrival of such ships as the
Archibald Russell, *L'Avenir* or *Pommern* attracted great local interest
and members of the public were allowed on board to see round
these romantic survivors of the great age of ocean sail.

After Bridge Wharf closed to steamer traffic in 1969 Prince's Dock
was used for a time for early season charters of Clyde steamers.

Ŋ Yorkhill Quay

This quay ran downriver for two or three hundred yards from the
Queen's Dock entrance. It was the point of departure for the Anchor
Line's weekly service to Boston and New York. Unlike other lines
such as Cunard, the Anchor Line catered for emigrant traffic rather
than the luxury trade. To meet its demands Anchor Line built five
large liners – *Caledonia*, *Transylvania*, *California*, *Cameronia*, *and
Tuscania* in the 1920s. With the coming of the Great Depression the
United States imposed a quota system on emigration and this had
serious effects on the emigrant trade. The *Tuscania* was transferred
to the company's Indian run. In April 1929 *Tuscania* arrived at
Yorkhill Quay during the Easter Holidays. Several cases of smallpox
were found on board and while the ship was isolated in quarantine
the victims were transferred to the city's Ruchill Hospital which
specialised in tropical and infectious diseases.

In the Summer months the Anchor Line also offered cruises from
the Clyde to the Hebrides and on occasions longer cruises to the
Mediterranean, for example in July 1935 they were advertising

Caledonia (1925). *Invertest* (1920), fuelling from a bunkering lighter alongside.

an August cruise in their liner *Britannia*. She was advertised to leave Glasgow on 2nd August, calling at Belfast, Barcelona, Messina, Athens, Cattaro, Tangier and returning to Glasgow on 28th August. Twenty five days of cruising were offered for the fairly modest sum, even in 1935, of 32 guineas (£33.60). For those with less time and money a fourteen day cruise, departing from Glasgow on 31st July, was offered on the *Tuscania* for 13 guineas (£13.65), The Anchor Line maintained its own tender, the screw steamer *Paladin*, which normally lay at the upriver end of Yorkhill Quay.

Yorkhill Quay is currently the base for the Clyde Maritime Trust and their sailing ship *Glenlee*. The *Glenlee* was built in 1896 at the Port Glasgow yard of Anderson Rodger & Company for Glasgow owners, Sterling & Company. A three masted barque, 245 feet 6 inches long, 1613 tons, she is now unique as the only Clyde-built sailing ship still afloat and available for restoration and preservation in the river of her birth. When built she was typical of the last age of sail, bulk carriers for long haul routes. In her later life she was in the service of the Spanish Navy as a sail training ship and renamed *Galatea*. She was bought by the Clyde Maritime Trust in 1992 and towed from Seville to the Clyde where she was dry-docked and surveyed. An appeal has been launched for her restoration to her state as she would have been seen in around the 1920s and to preserve her as a tangible link with the Clyde's great age of sailing ship construction and Scotland's great age of owner-ship of sailing ships.

Ŷ Yorkhill Basin

This extension of Yorkhill Quay was used by two Liverpool shipping lines – T. & J. Brocklebank and the Blue Funnel Line. Brocklebank's ships were particularly handsome vessels and their distinctive black funnel with a blue and white band was well known on the river. Their main trade was as "jute clippers" – sailing between Calcutta and Glasgow. The basin was used by the Blue Funnel Line until the opening of the King George V Dock.

Yorkhill was also used by what was jocularly called the "Grey Funnel Line" – the Royal Navy. During the Second World War the County Class cruiser *Sussex* was bombed here during an air raid in September 1940. The *Sussex* had come into the Clyde to have a turbine re-bladed and was ready to sail when in the early morning of 18th September a 250 pound bomb hit her and ignited her oil fuel. The fire that resulted threatened the ships ammunition magazines and 2000 residents in the neighbourhood and patients in the nearby Yorkhill Hospital were evacuated until the fire was brought under control. Among the more unlikely participants that came to the aid of the *Sussex* was one of the Clyde's vehicular ferries which acted as a platform for fire fighting equipment. *Sussex* took two years to rebuild in Alexander Stephen's yard at Linthouse after this attack. Yorkhill was used latterly for laid up vessels, including the ferries of the Isle of Man Steam Packet Company and Sealink.

Up to 1939 the largest regular visitor to Glasgow docks was *Ceramic* of the Shaw Savill line. This 20,000 ton ship, originally built for the White Star line, regularly berthed at Yorkhill Basin.

Ŝ Govan Graving Docks

Built for the Clyde Navigation Trust between 1869 and 1898 this complex of three dry docks was extensively used by Clyde steamers for winter refits and annual overhauls. The first dock, opened in 1875, is 565 feet long and 72 feet wide with a second, and larger dock following in 1886. They are still in existence but closed in 1988. There are plans to restore these extremely evocative and important relics of an older river to form the site for a museum of ships and shipbuilding and to allow preserved ships to be seen on the river of their birth. The adjacent wet basin was formerly Harland & Wolff's and later Alexander Stephen's fitting out berth.

Empress of Canada (1922) in Govan Graving Dock.

℞ Kelvinhaugh Ferry

This ferry ran from Stag Lane, near the Govan Graving Dock to Yorkhill on the North bank. It was a particularly busy ferry on Saturday afternoons when Rangers were playing a home match at their nearby Ibrox stadium. In an earlier period this had been a triangular ferry route, incorporating a call at Stobcross Quay. The Kelvinhaugh Ferry ceased to operate in the early 1980s.

⚓ Harland & Wolff Shipyard

The large red brick engine shed of Harland & Wolff's shipyard is all that now remains of what was one of the most historic and significant of the Glasgow yards. Modern iron shipbuilding started at Govan when, in 1841, Robert Napier took over a small wooden shipyard, Govan Old Yard and developed a new large scale enterprise there. He later moved to the Govan East Yard. Napier, who became known as "the father of Clyde shipbuilding" both from the innovative nature and the high quality of his work and from the number of leading shipbuilders who trained under him, produced some of the Clyde's finest vessels from his Govan yards. Napier's commitment to quality is demonstrated in a letter he wrote to Samuel Cunard in 1839:

> I cannot, and will not admit of anything being done or introduced into these engines but what I am satisfied is sound and good.

Among the "firsts" launched from Napier's Govan yard were: the first iron paddle-steamers for the Royal Navy. Indeed for a long time Napier was the leading Clyde builder for the Royal Navy – building many pioneering vessels including the experimental screw frigate HMS *Simoon*, and the early ironclad HMS *Black Prince* launched in 1861. Napier's yard also built the world's first train ferry – the *Leviathan* of 1849 for the Granton – Burntisland crossing. When he launched the Cunarder *Persia* in 1855 she was at that time the world's largest ship and the first Cunarder for the transatlantic mail service to be built in iron. After her trials in January 1856 the owners' representative said that:

> Mr Napier had built forty large vessels for the Company's lines, and there had never been a fault or a mistake from the starting to the carrying out of any one of them.

Napier's contribution to the development of Clyde shipbuilding and engineering cannot be over-estimated. The Clyde became the world's most important centre of shipbuilding – as late as the 1950's the river was still producing approximately one seventh of the total tonnage of sea-going ships in the world. When the history of the yards that produced this tonnage is told, a recurring theme in very many of them is the contribution that had been made by men who had learned their business under the tutelage of Robert Napier.

On Napier's death in 1876, what had been a family concern was sold to a group headed by A. C. Kirk, one of Napier's former apprentices. After Kirk's death the company was bought over by Beardmore and operations moved down-river to Dalmuir. In 1912 the major Belfast-based shipbuilders Harland & Wolff, the builders of the *Olympic* and her ill-fated sister ship *Titanic*, decided to expand and bought the three Govan yards, redeveloping them to create what became one of the Clyde's showpiece yards.

Harland & Wolff's output was varied, including naval vessels, tankers and cargo ships. For example the Union Castle Line came to Harland & Wolff for a series of four motorships, *Llangibby Castle*, (1929), *Dunbar Castle* and *Winchester Castle* (1930) and *Warwick Castle* (1931). The yard's only contribution to the Clyde steamer fleet was the 1932 turbine steamer *Duchess of Hamilton*, a handsome vessel which remained in service until 1970.

The Harland & Wolff yard closed in 1962 after a period of decline. Capital investment in new plant and machinery had for some time been concentrated on the company's main yard in Belfast and the Govan yard was no longer able to compete effectively in the contemporary market place with its demand for ever-larger ships.

The Harland & Wolff engine shed is now occasionally used for large scale theatrical performances – appropriately enough the first production, in 1990, was Bill Bryden's epic celebration of the Clyde's shipbuilding tradition – *The Ship*.

Llangibby Castle , Union Castle Line (1929), 1950

Duchess of Hamilton (1932) passing Anderston Quay, early 1960's.

Ň River Kelvin

Just beyond Yorkhill Basin the River Kelvin, now silted up, enters the Clyde. The paddle steamer *Waverley* was built here at the Pointhouse yard of A. & J. Inglis on the upstream bank of the Kelvin. She was launched on 2nd October 1946 and was the second Craigendoran steamer to bear this name. She proved, in the event, to be the last ship built for the L.N.E.R. Craigendoran service. Eleven of the company's paddle steamers were built at this yard, from the *Meg Merrilies* of 1866 and including such famous names as the *Kenilworth* and *Marmion*. In addition the *Lincoln Castle* was built here for L.N.E.R.'s Humber Service. Unusually one of these ships came back to her builders to be scrapped, this was the *Kenilworth*, built here in 1898 and scrapped forty years later in 1938.

The Craigendoran fleet was nationalised in 1948 under the British Railways' flag. The *Waverley* (1947) and *Jeanie Deans* (1931) returned to Pointhouse for their annual winter refits up to 1962 when the Inglis yard closed. Inglis, apart from their specialisation in river steamers also produced tugs and small coasters. From 1919 onwards the Inglis yard formed part of the Harland & Wolff Group, as eventually also did the Meadowside shipyard of D. & W. Henderson, on the opposite, downriver side of the Kelvin.

Waverley (1899) approaching Craigmore – post 1920.

Waverley and *Jeanie Deans* in the Kelvin with a Maid class vessel on the slip.
Waverley is at Inglis and *Jeanie Deans* at Henderson.

The Meadowside yard lies in one of the oldest steamship building centres of the Clyde. The first yard established here was that of
Tod & MacGregor. Both partners had formerly worked for Robert
Napier, and after some years in business at Mavisbank Quay set
up their premises here in 1847. Early photographs exist of their
paddle-steamer *Juno* fitting out there for the American Civil War.
The *Juno*, built in 1860 was, like quite a number of other fast Clyde
steamers of the period, secretly bought by agents of the
Confederate States of America and used in an attempt to beat the
Federal Government's blockade of the South during the Civil War.
Meadowside was also the site of the Clyde's first major dry dock –
built by Tod & MacGregor here in 1856.

After the Tod & MacGregor period the yard was taken over by
D. & W. Henderson in association with the Anchor Line. For the
Anchor Line the yard produced, among many other ships, the
North Atlantic passenger liner *Columbia* in 1902. This ship was a
very familiar part of the Clyde scene with her Saturday afternoon
departures from Yorkhill Quay for New York – so familiar and
regular was this sailing that she even entered the world of fiction.
When Neil Munro's puffer *Vital Spark* sailed up river her skipper,
Para Handy, was plagued by

. . .brats of boys that come to the riverside when we'll be going
up the Clyde at Yoker and cry '*Columbia*, ahoy' at us – the
duvvles own!

Columbia (1902)

For river services, the yard built, in 1880, the *Ivanhoe* for the idiosyncratically named Frith of Clyde Steam Packet Company's service to Arran and the lower Firth. The distinguishing feature of the *Ivanhoe* was that she was built and managed as a teetotal boat. The absence of licensing regulations on board Clyde steamers meant that there was often a considerable problem of drunken and unruly behaviour on board – not for nothing is "steamboats" a Glasgow euphemism for drunkenness! The owners of *Ivanhoe* shrewdly reckoned that there was a market for a temperance boat and indeed the late nineteenth century saw an enormous growth in the temperance movement with organisations such as the Rechabites and the Band of Hope recruiting vigorously and successfully among young and old alike. These principled objectors to the demon drink as well as the more genteel class of passenger who did not wish to mix with the nineteenth century equivalent of the lager lout formed the *Ivanhoe's* clientele. After 1897 she was taken over by the Caledonian Steam Packet Company – and swiftly succumbed to drink!

Other famous Clyde steamers built here included the handsome *Lord of the Isles* launched in 1891 for M. T. Clark's Glasgow & Inveraray Steamboat Company and placed on their Glasgow to Inveraray service. She was bought in 1912 by Williamson Buchanan Turbine Steamers Ltd and in their service she left Glasgow at 10.30 a.m. for Dunoon, Rothesay, Tighnabruaich, then cruising round Bute and back to Glasgow. She was much missed when eventually she was broken up in 1928.

Ivanhoe (1880) leaving Rothesay.

Lord of the Isles (1891)

Among the more unusual contracts won by D. & W. Henderson was that for the racing yacht *Britannia* built in 1893 for the Prince of Wales (later Edward VII) – this splendid vessel was also raced by George V who shared with his father a great enthusiasm for yacht racing.

The long story of shipbuilding at Meadowside ended with the closure of Henderson's yard in 1935. The end came in July 1935 after the launch of the *Inventor* for T. & J. Harrison of Liverpool.

§ Kvaerner Govan

The last merchant shipbuilder on the upper river. Like many Clyde yards this has had many identities. Shipbuilding began on the site of Fairfield Farm in 1864 by Randolph, Elder & Company, the leading figure in the firm being John Elder, yet another "old boy" of Robert Napier's yard, the pioneer of the compound engine and one of the leading marine engineers of his day. After Elder's death in 1869 a new partnership was established under the name of John Elder & Company. From 1884 Elder's and Robert Napier's were recognised by the Admiralty as being the two Clyde yards capable of building the largest naval vessels and were on the permanent tendering list for machinery for ships built in Royal Navy Dockyards. In 1888 the company was reconstructed as the Fairfield Shipbuilding and Engineering Company Ltd.

One of the most unusual ships built during the Elder period was the *Livadia* – a royal yacht for the Tsar of Russia. The previous Russian royal yacht having been sunk this ship was designed with both Imperial comfort and Imperial safety in mind and was generally described as being shaped like a turbot, being 285 feet long and 153 feet wide. Based on the design of circular battleships invented by the Russian Admiral Popoff the *Livadia* created a sensation. Neil Munro, then a Glasgow journalist, wrote:

"There have been many curious craft of an experimental character built in Clyde shipyards, but the oddest of all was undoubtedly the *Livadia*. She was launched at Fairfield on Wednesday, July 7, 1880, by the firm of John Elder & Company, and created as much sensation as if she had been a flying submarine. Never was more demand for tickets to see a launching ceremony; there were privileged guests and newspaper correspondents from every maritime part of the country, even from the Continent and America."

Fortunately the oddness of the *Livadia* can still be judged from a splendid model in the Glasgow Museum of Transport.

The variety and extent of the work handled by a yard like Fairfield at the height of the Clyde's fame is suggested by this listing from 1912:

In Building Berths – ss *Calgarian* for Allan Line Steamship Co.; *Empress of Asia* and *Empress of Russia* for Canadian Pacific Railway Co. and five Torpedo Boat Destroyers for the Admiralty. In Fitting-out Basin – H.M. Cruiser *New Zealand* for Admiralty, and ss *Ermine* for G. & J. Burns Ltd.

It is hardly necessary to point out that this total of twelve ships from one yard is several times the total output of the entire river today.

Between the wars Fairfield, the largest Glasgow shipyard, became part of the Lithgow shipbuilding group and later became part of Upper Clyde Shipbuilders. In 1972 Govan Shipbuilders was formed out of the UCS crash and the yard was sold in 1988 to the Norwegian shipbuilder and engineering company Kvaerner.

The Elder name is still prominent in Govan due to the legacies of John Elder's wife Isabella – the Elder Park provides a large and popular recreational area and the more intellectual needs of the citizens are served by the Elder Park Library. Among Lady Elder's other benefactions was a Chair of Naval Architecture at Glasgow University.

Among the many river steamers built at Fairfield was the 1903 *Duchess of Fife* which after a long career, including service in the two world wars, was scrapped in 1953. In 1931 Fairfield also built one of the best-loved of the Clyde steamers, *Jeanie Deans*, for the L.N.E.R.'s Craigendoran to Loch Long service. After war service *Jeanie Deans* came back to the Clyde and continued to ply until 1964. She was sold to the Coastal Steam Packet Company who bravely tried to revive the paddle steamer trade on he Thames. She survived there for the 1966 and 1967 summer seasons, but ran for a total of only twenty eight days in these two seasons. She was sold for breaking-up in Belgium in late 1967. The 1935 Gourock to Holy Loch paddler *Marchioness of Lorne* and the 1936 Arran turbine steamer *Marchioness of Graham* were other Fairfield

Jeanie Deans leaving Fairfield for trials, May 1931.

Jeanie Deans leaving Dunoon, the *Duchess of Argyll* sailing from Wemyss Bay and the *Eagle III* from Rothesay. (1931)

Marchoness of Lorne (1935). Launched 19/2/35.

favourites. In 1937 the yard launched the twin paddle steamers *Juno* and *Jupiter* for the Caledonian Steam Packet Company's Gourock based services. *Juno* was lost while performing war service as an anti-aircraft ship.

A feature of the yard was its reputation for fast building. For example the *Duchess of Fife* was laid down on 17th January, launched on 9th May and was on her trials by 5th June. Such a schedule was only attainable by a company policy of continually upgrading facilities and investing in new plant and machinery.

Away from the Clyde the Fairfield yard was famed for the large passenger liners it built. The *Athenia*, which has already been referred to, was a Fairfield ship, launched in 1922. It was part of a major building programme to replace wartime losses in passenger liners. Fairfield fully shared in this with *Athenia* and *Letitia* for Donaldson Line, *Tuscania* and *Transylvania* for Anchor Line and *Empress of Canada* and *Montrose* for Canadian Pacific. Two years later one of the early diesel electric ships the *Aorangi* for the New Zealand Shipping Company's service between New Zealand, Honolulu and Vancouver came from Fairfield. In 1930 the yard launched the *Empress of Japan* – a handsome white hulled three-funnelled ship for service between Vancouver and Yokohama. This ship held the Blue Riband of the Pacific for the fastest time on this route. Her speed and capacity ensured that she was commandeered for service as a troop ship on the outbreak of war. On Japan's entry to the war she was renamed *Empress of Scotland*, and in her post-war career she was to be a familiar site on the Clyde sailing between Scotland and Canada carrying emigrants and the brides of Canadian servicemen to start a new life across the Atlantic. A series of fine ships for the Anchor Line, *Circassia* (1937), *Cilicia* (1938), and *Caledonia* (1948) – also came from Fairfield.

One of the typically close Clyde yard connections with a shipping firm, in Fairfield's case with the Liverpool & North Wales Steamship Company, saw a regular output of vessels for the owners – these included the *St. Seirol* and *St Tudno*.

Empress of Japan – fitting out at Fairfield. (1930)

The yard latterly turned its hand to building ferries such as the *Wahine* in 1965 for the Union Steamship Company of New Zealand. *Wahine* had just entered service when she was unfortunately lost in an accident in Auckland Harbour. In 1987 the yard launched the 40,000 ton *Norsea* for North Sea Ferries Ltd. – the largest ship built on Clyde since *QE2* and at that time the world's largest car ferry.

Kvaerner have built several gas tankers in recent years and HMS *Ocean*, a helicopter carrier, built in conjunction with the Barrow-in-Furness yard of VSEL for the Royal Navy.

The Govan area with yards like Harland's, Fairfield and Linthouse further down river is all now inextricably linked with shipbuilding. It is however as well to remember that the development of shipbuilding on this stretch of the river came quite late in the history of the Clyde. In 1851 a local writer, Hugh MacDonald, could note that:

> The walk from Govan to Renfrew, a distance of some four miles along the margin of the river, is in the highest degree pleasing. . . On both sides the country is somewhat flat, partaking in this respect, as well as in its general fertility, more of the softer character of English landscape. . . An abundance of trees and hedgerows still further heightens the illusion so that we could. . . almost fancy ourselves rambling through some genial scene in "merry England".

In ten or fifteen years after this was written the river scene MacDonald described so picturesquely had been totally transformed and the industrialisation of the Clyde had moved inexorably onwards.

⚘N Meadowside Granary

On the North bank of the river can be seen the striking thirteen-storey red brick buildings of the Meadowside Granaries. Ships from many countries once used this facility but in particular it was associated with the importation of grain from Canada. The Granaries were, like so much of the riverside scene, the creation of the Clyde Navigation Trust and the first part of this massive complex was built in 1911-1913. The site had previously been a football pitch, the ground of Partick Thistle Football Club. Supporters still tell how, if the home team were finding things difficult, extra time could be ensured by kicking the ball from the pitch into the Clyde – not an option which the Jags have now at their Firhill Stadium in Maryhill! An extension was completed in 1937 and two post war buildings complete the complex. Part of the granary was in recent years used for the storage of EC Intervention grain and for storing grain for distilling. The granary, said to be the largest brick-built building in Europe and to contain twenty million bricks, was finally closed in December 1995. The roof of the down river end of the Granary houses a Clydeport Control Tower.

The extent and importance that the grain trade of Glasgow once enjoyed is indicated by the figures for imports into the Port of Glasgow in 1887. In that year 209,228 tons of flour and 153,948 tons of Indian corn came into Glasgow – and only iron ore, at 374,826 tons, was a larger bulk cargo.

Today Meadowside Wharf is still operated by Clydeport and used for the handling of clean dry bulk cargoes. Typical products dealt with include grain for milling and distilling, material for conversion into animal feedstuff and fish meal for the production of food for the fish farming industry.

Merklands Lairage

Downstream from Meadowside Granary is the Merklands Lairage. Constructed in 1907 to handle the importation of cattle into the city to feed the ever-growing population of industrial Scotland. The Burns Laird ships brought large consignments of cattle into the city from Ireland to be processed in the many slaughterhouses along Old Dumbarton Road or to be moved to other areas by means of the network of railway lines which served the lairage complex.

Other than its use by cattle boats Merklands was used by the Clyde Shipping Company and also by the passenger vessels of Burns & Laird. In 1919 the Clydebank-built *Duchess of Rothesay*

Duchess of Rothesay (1895).

Duchess of Rothesay bieng raised after sinking at Merklands in 1919.

returned to the Clyde after war service as a minesweeper. She was sent to Barclay, Curle's yard for refit and while lying at Merklands Wharf sank on 1st June due to a sea cock having been left open. It took eight weeks to raise her with divers working in the thick mud of the river. However the *Duchess* survived and completed fifty years service, including a second spell as a minesweeper during the Second World War, before being scrapped in 1945.

Although the Lairage was closed for its designed trade around 1974 and has now been demolished the wharf itself is still used by small coasting vessels and is regularly visited by the tug *St Serf* and a barge bringing in gravel from Greenock and a concrete batching plant is located here.

℞ Whiteinch Ferry

Whiteinch was the site of both an elevating deck vehicle ferry and a passenger only ferry. Ferry No. 1 – the smallest of Clyde Trust's three high level vehicular ferries ran this route, in 1938 a fourth ferry was built to provide year round coverage when vessels had to be withdrawn for refit.

Whiteinch, as the name suggests ("Inch" being an old Scots word for an island), was once the site of one of the Clyde's islands. Before work started on widening and deepening the river there were six of these inches in the stretch between the city centre and the mouth of the Cart at Renfrew. One was opposite Carlton Place; one, the "Water Inch" at the mouth of the Kelvin; one here – the

"White Inch"; "Buck Inch" a little downstream; the "King's Inch" at Elderslie and the "Sand Inch" at Renfrew.

℞ Clyde Tunnel

The road tunnel under the Clyde from Whiteinch on the North Bank to Linthouse on the South Bank runs immediately beyond the end of Merklands Wharf. This replacement for earlier ferry services was built between 1957 and 1964. Its planning dates back to the immediate post-war period with a still busy river and harbour, when a tunnel, which would not interfere with river traffic, was seen as a better option than a bridge.

℗ Alexander Stephen of Linthouse

The site of yet another vanished shipyard lies just downstream from the Clyde Tunnel crossing. This company, moved to Kelvinhaugh on the Clyde in the 1850s from earlier premises in various East Coast ports. In its period at Kelvinhaugh they built 147 ships, one of which, the *Otago*, an iron barque built in 1869, was later to be the first command of the Polish-born novelist Joseph Conrad. The quality of the Clyde built vessel was praised by Conrad who described her in *The Shadow Line*:

> Her hull, her rigging, filled my eye with great content. . . At the first glance I saw that she was a high-class vessel, a harmonious creature in the lines of her fine body, in the proportioned tallness of her spars. Whatever her age and history, she had preserved the stamp of her origin.

Stephen's lease of the Kelvinhaugh yard was due to expire in 1871 and an alternative site was found down-river at Linthouse. This property was bought in 1868 and in the next year work began to lay it out as a modern shipyard. The first launch from the new yard came in 1870 with the steam ship *Glendarroch* for Glasgow owners. A large number of very fine ships were to follow her down the slips at this yard. Although the new yard started its account with the launch of a steam ship much of their output in the 1870s and 80s continued to be sailing vessels. In this century notable vessels from the yard included the 1928 *Viceroy of India* – an early turbo-electric ship for P&O. Among important post-war launches were the *Olympia* for the Greek Line in 1953 and the handsome *Aureol* for Elder Dempster's West Africa service. Apart from large passenger liners like those mentioned above, and *Caledonia* (1925)

The liner *Olympia* built 1953 by Stephen of Linthouse.

and *California* (1923) for the Anchor Line, a staple business of the yard was the construction of banana boats for Elders & Fyffe. These fast cargo vessels bringing the banana crop from the West Indies also carried a limited number of passengers and many discriminating passengers felt that a voyage on a banana boat represented one of the most pleasurable forms of sea-travel.

Stephen & Sons were also major Admiralty contractors. The sloop *Amethyst* (1943) which made a famous escape down the Yangtse River under the guns of the Chinese Communists in 1949, an exploit which became the subject of a well-known film, was a Stephen's ship. During the Second World War the yard launched the cruisers, *Kenya* and *Ceylon*, the aircraft carrier *Ocean*, the minelayers *Manxman* and *Ariadne*, fast ships with a speed of forty knots as well as a range of other destroyers, escort vessels and minesweepers.

The Linthouse yard was also the location for one of the most tragic incidents on the Clyde – the launch of the steam coaster *Daphne* in July 1883. *Daphne* was launched in a high state of completion with engines on board, but the boiler was not fitted and a large deck opening was left to allow this to be done during the fitting out phase. Two hundred workmen remained on board during the launch so that they could continue to work while the *Daphne* was being towed upstream to her fitting-out berth. Immediately on being launched the ship heeled to port and then completely rolled over. 124 of those on board were drowned and the subsequent investigation found that the ship's design had led to an instability which was compounded by the weight of men and gear on deck and by the inrush of water through the boiler access when the deck came under water level.

The Yard closed in 1968 and the site now houses the long-established Glasgow optical firm of Barr & Stroud, now known as Pilkington Optronics (Barr & Stroud), among whose products are naval and military rangefinders, submarine periscopes etc.

Shieldhall Sewage Works

Reference has already been made to the problems caused by the discharge of the city's sewage and waste into the Clyde and the part that this played in making "all the way" sailings less popular. The City Corporation built a sewage treatment works at Dalmarnock in 1894 which was capable of treating the sewage of a quarter of the city, extended this with a plant at Dalmuir in 1904 and the Shieldhall Works in 1910. This purified the liquid discharges into the river but the treated sewage sludge had to be removed and to achieve this the City Council established its own fleet of sludge vessels. These still leave on regular down-river trips each day to dump the treated solid waste in deep water off Garroch Head, at the southern end of the Island of Bute. The first ship bought for this purpose was the *Dalmuir* – which was converted to this role from an oil tanker. In 1910 the specially designed *Shieldhall* was built and she was to be followed by *Dalmarnock (I)* of 1925 ,

Dalmarnock (1925)

S.S. Shieldhall at Shieldhall Sewage Works, 3/9/60.

Shieldhall (II) of 1955 and a new *Dalmarnock* of 1970 (which resulted in the 1925 *Dalmarnock* being renamed *Dalmarnock II*) and, the most recent addition to the fleet, the *Garroch Head* of 1978. *Shieldhall (II)* is now preserved on the Solent.

Despite their unappealing cargoes these ships have always been popular with shipping enthusiasts and a sail down-river on one of these vessels has been a much sought-after privilege. When Glasgow and the Clyde celebrated the centenary of the *Comet* in 1912 two vessels were used to transport the official party downstream from the Broomielaw to the shipping review at the Tail of the Bank. MacBrayne's flagship, the *Columba*, carried the representatives of the local authorities and other public bodies while the humble sludge boat *Shieldhall* conveyed:

"A party, representative of the shipbuilding industry; consisting of Shipwrights, Engineers, Boilermakers and other trades. . . ".

Indeed the sludge boats and the *Waverley* are now the only regular "all the way" sailings. However the long term future of these vessels is likely to be affected by a European Directive prohibiting the dumping of waste at sea after 1998. By that time a new disposal strategy will require to be found and the *Dalmarnock* and the *Garroch Head*, which by that time will be the responsibility of the new West of Scotland Water Authority, will have either to be disposed of or found a new role – possibly in the tourism field.

The success of sewage treatment and, it must be admitted, the decline of heavy industry on the Clyde, has resulted in recent years in the river attaining a state of cleanliness and purity which it had lacked for two centuries. Salmon and trout are to be seen again in the city reaches of the Clyde and in once noxious tributaries such as the Kelvin although it may be thought unlikely that the salmon and trout fishing on the Clyde and its tributaries will ever regain its former importance. In 1790 the minister of Dumbarton could write of the Leven fishings:

> Salmon and trout are taken in large quantities. The former frequently sells so high as 1s 6d per lb. . . Trout generally sells at 4d per pound. Very large eels, and a large species of flounder, are often caught by the salmon-fishers. A species of sea animals, most destructive of the salmon, are almost every summer season found in numbers, playing in the Clyde off the castle; they go up sometimes two miles higher. . . These are called. . . porpoises. The salmon fishery employs 16 men.

N Charles Connell

This Scotstoun yard had a history of over 100 years from its foundation in 1861 up to its incorporation into Upper Clyde Shipbuilders in 1968. Among the regular customers of this yard were T. & J. Harrison, J. & J. Denholm, P. Henderson and Company and above all the Edinburgh-based Ben Line, for whom no fewer than forty-eight ships were built. In the earlier part of the yard's history they were noted as builders of sailing ships, especially China tea clippers.

S Shieldhall Riverside Berths

This wharf was used for vessels carrying slab steel for Ravenscraig until the demise of the Lanarkshire steel industry. It is now used for small fertiliser cargoes. Occasionally larger vessels may be seen here and this berth is also used for ships involved in the export of scrap metal.

S King George V Dock

This major dock was the last of the Clyde's docks to be built. Unlike the earlier Prince's and Queen's Docks it is a large single basin with unrestricted entry, designed to be easily usable by the increasingly large vessels which were then trading into the Clyde. It was opened 1931 by King George V who, appropriately enough,

King George V (1926) at the opening of the King George V Dock by H. M. King George V on 15/7/31.

sailed down river from Bridge Wharf (just below King George V Bridge) on the Denny-built turbine steamer *King George V*. The steamer, turning into the basin, broke a tape and so inaugurated the new dock. KGV Dock was planned to be the first of a new series of dock developments on the South Bank, however further docks proved not required due to the depression of the pre-war period and the changing trade patterns of the post-war years. The area to the West of the Docks was earmarked for expansion and in July 1935 the Clyde Navigation Trust had under consideration a £7 million plan for an additional 4½ miles of wharfage to cater for what they felt would be the city's needs for the next fifty years. At the same time they were planning the construction of an industrial estate adjacent to the Docks to attract new industry to the Clyde. Downstream from the Docks, at Braehead, a coal-fired power station was built after the Second World War – this has since been demolished and the site is to be redeveloped as a business and retail park. Among the companies who used King George V Dock were Blue Star Line, Blue Funnel and Clan Line.

Today King George V Dock and the associated Shieldhall Riverside Quay is the main area of dock activity in the City of Glasgow. Clydeport offer a wide range of facilities here for importers and exporters, including shed accommodation, paved areas for marshalling cargoes, dockside and mobile cranes. The dock is regularly used by many foreign going ships – especially British and Russian vessels and caters for traffic in imported commodities such as steel pipes, cement, animal feeds and the export of steel plate, scrap metal and engineering products.

King George V Dock. The *Clan Buchanan* under tow.
Photo: Hunting Aerofilms Ltd.

⇑N Yarrow Shipbuilders

At Scotstoun on the North Bank of the River can be found the last
specialist warship yard on the Clyde. Yarrow moved to Glasgow
from the Thames in 1906 to what was then a "green field" site.
Yarrow had let it be known that they wished to move from London
and received over four hundred offers of sites or enquiries from
all over the British Isles. Scotstoun was chosen, because as Alfred
Yarrow observed:

> When you want apples, you go to Covent Garden; for meat to a
> meat market, and for ships you go to the North.

Yarrow, along with John Brown at Clydebank, Fairfield, Stephen
at Linthouse, Beardmore at Dalmuir, Denny of Dumbarton and
Scott of Greenock, formed the core of warship building capacity

on the Clyde. In peacetime these firms had most of the naval contracts although in a wartime emergency, of course, all yards found themselves pressed into service. Much naval work for the Clyde consisted in supplying machinery for naval vessels built in one of the Royal Dockyards – these had a hull building capacity but no engine building facilities.

The dominance of the specialist warship yards is shown by the production figures for naval vessels during the First World War – the Clyde launched almost 760,000 tons of warships between 1914 and 1918, two thirds of this tonnage coming from six yards – Clydebank, Fairfield, Dalmuir, Yarrow, Scott and Denny. The three largest naval yards – Fairfield, John Brown and Beardmore – on the outbreak of war became Admiralty controlled dockyards and were not allowed to start any merchant ship construction during the wartime period.

Yarrow Shipbuilders now act as the lead yard for the Royal Navy Type-23 frigates and for the projected Euro-frigate planned for the twenty-first century. The yard also built frigates, corvettes and patrol vessels for foreign navies as well as carrying out some commercial work. The yard, which has a large covered construction hall, took over the adjacent Blythswood Shipbuilding and Engineering Company in 1960 and also absorbed the Elderslie Dry docks which were much used for refitting coastal vessels. Yarrow Shipbuilders is now owned by the GEC Group which also owns the Barrow-in-Furness submarine builder VSEL.

Although historically the company's lifeblood has always been naval construction they have at times produced other vessels such

mv *Maid of Ashton* (1953) arriving at Gourock.

as the 1953 mv *Maid of Ashton*, which is now moored on the Thames as the floating restaurant *Hispaniola*. Yard apprentices built the yacht *Southern Cross* in the 1960s and an unusual product was a series of ferries for services on the African Lakes. These were pre-fabricated at Scotstoun and shipped to Africa in parts for erection on site. In the winter season of 1956/57 Yarrow re-boilered the Clyde turbine steamer *Queen Mary II*. This popular steamer had been launched in 1933 at Denny's of Dumbarton as *Queen Mary* but when, in the following year, John Brown's launched No. 534, the Clyde steamer's owners agreed to add II to her name to allow the Cunard liner to carry the unadorned title *Queen Mary*.

Navigation Works

Renfrew, on the South Bank, houses the maintenance base for vessels of Clyde Navigation Trust and this is still used as repair yard for small vessels. The Navigation Works opened in 1908, replacing an earlier base downriver at Dalmuir which had been sold to William Beardmore to form part of their new warship building yard.

Renfrew Harbour

Colloquially known as the "Pudzeoch", so named from the Pudzeoch Burn which flows into Clyde at this point. The Harbour is still used as a winter lay-up base for small motor vessels and yachts. It has served as a calling place for the *Balmoral* on her down river cruises. One of the former Erskine and Renfrew ferry vessels is preserved in the Pudzeoch and is owned by the Renfrew Historical Society.

Renfrew Ferry

A vehicular ferry formerly ran across between Renfrew and Yoker on the North Bank. A chain hauled ferry, originally steam driven but latterly diesel powered, operated here from 1868. The service had originally been run by the Burgh of Renfrew but was taken over by the Clyde Navigation Trust in 1911.

Renfrew Ferry ceased functioning as a car ferry in 1984 although a passenger service is now operated by two specially built ferries *Renfrew Rose* and *Yoker Swan*. These ships, built at Ardrossan, although operating solely as passenger ferries have the capacity to carry an ambulance in the case of emergencies.

The power lines across the river were erected in 1929 in connection with a power station being built at Yoker.

Vehicular Ferryboat No.4 (1938) in the Pudzeoch.

Renfrew Ferry (1952)

Yoker Swan (1984).

Ps *Eagle III* (1910) in her first season, passing Renfrew. The former Renfrew Wharf can be seen beyond the Ferry Green.

ʂ Ferry Green

This open space downstream from the Ferry offers a good vantage point for observing traffic on the river. The preserved engine, made in Robert Napier's Lancefield Works, of the paddle tug *Clyde*, which was built for the Clyde Navigation Trust by A. & J. Inglis, Pointhouse, in 1851, may be seen here. Downstream was the former Renfrew Wharf – hit by a landmine in the Blitz of March 1941.

ʂ Simons Lobnitz

Two specialist firms of dredger builder were established at Renfrew. First on this site was William Simons & Company who moved across the river from Whiteinch in 1860. Then in 1874 Lobnitz, Coulborn & Company (later Lobnitz & Company) established here on an adjacent site. The two firms amalgamated under the familiar title of Simons Lobnitz in 1957. The firm was taken over by the Weir Group in 1959 but sadly they were forced to close in 1963. Their last vessel was a large Russian suction dredger, a model of which in the Glasgow Museum of Transport serves as a reminder of what was once an important aspect of the Clyde's production. William Simons built their first hopper barge for the Clyde Navigation Trust in 1862 and thereafter they were major suppliers of these vessels. Until that year the Trust had dumped the spoil from the river along the banks or downriver below Dumbarton, but in 1862 their new fleet of hopper barges started

The Common Old Hopper "wi' a number instead o' a name".
No.4 off Dumbarton in 1962.

taking the dredged material to a dump site in Loch Long. However, in time, the residents on Loch Long-side complained about this practice and the Trust had to move their disposal site to deep water three miles South of Garroch Head.

Unlike the dredgers, which eventually rejoiced in names like *Cairndhu* and *Rosslyn*, these hard-working hopper barges had to be content with numbers: or perhaps not content, if J. J. Bell's poem, *Song of an Old Hopper*, is to be believed:

> I'm only a hopper, an old style o' hopper,
> Wi' a number in place o' a name –
> Which is surely a sin an' a shame.
> Why! the grandest o' ships, the very tip-topper,
> 'Ud be nothin' a-wantin' a name!
> But I'm only a hopper, a humble old hopper,
> Wi' never a chance o' fame.

> But it's want o' a name, that sticks most in my throat.
> An' at Greenock down yonder they keeps a wee boat
> For to ask at all ships if they've sickness below –
> A saucy, impiddent wee puffer – an' oh!
> When I sees the "Nathaniel Dunlop" . . .that is when
> I feels I could sink! – me that's just No. 10! . . .

The last of the "humble old hoppers" on the river were numbers 25 and 26, the last of the steam-powered hoppers and numbers 27 and 28, the final two diesel powered hoppers. There has been, with the decline in river traffic, a reduction in recent years in dredging activity upstream from Yarrow's. This has presented problems not only for potential river traffic but also threatened to obstruct sewage and storm water outfalls into the river. Recently the local authorities and Clydeport have agreed to jointly fund a dredging programme from Bridge Wharf to Yarrow's at a cost of £270,000. This work, apart from its other advantages will keep the *Waverley's* berth at Anderston Quay operational for a few more years.

Like many of the Clyde yards the Simons Lobnitz premises had had numerous previous occupants and in the mid nineteenth century one of their predecessors was the firm of J. Henderson & Sons whose output included steamers like the *Ruby* which took part in the highly competitive trade between the Broomielaw and Rothesay. So competitive was this route that the *Ruby* and her rivals such as *Rothesay Castle* raced each other so as to be first at each point of call, and so scoop up the cream of the traffic. Indeed in the nineteenth century the problem of steamer racing attracted much popular and official attention. Contests between crack ships and their proud skippers in open waters were one thing, but the tendency to take risks and ignore the rules of the road in striving to beat a rival to a pier often resulted in collisions and the inevitable sequel of court appearances and fines for the offending captains.

After the Lobnitz yard closed their basin was used as a small yacht repair yard and is now used as a scrapyard and also by a number of coasting vessels trading to Spanish ports.

Yoker

Just opposite Simons Lobnitz and removed to make way for Rothesay Dock was the Yoker Shipyard of Napier Shanks & Bell. Founded by a grandson of the great Robert Napier the firm established themselves here in 1877 and among many other ships built the first two paddle steamers to be designed for the Glasgow & South Western Railway Company – the *Neptune*

Barclay Curle's Elderslie dry dock with troopship *Dunera* in dock and *Queen Mary II* on river wall.
Photo: Hunting Aerofilms Ltd.

P.S. *Neptune* (1892) arriving at Rothesay c. 1912/14.

Typical river view, *Eagle III* (1910) passing Yoker.

and *Mercury* of 1892. The Glasgow & South Western had commenced shipping operations in the Autumn of 1891 and was forced, as a temporary expedient, to purchase second-hand vessels until its new ships became available.

The Yoker yard, by now renamed Napier & Miller, closed in 1906 and transferred down-river to Old Kilpatrick.

⚲ Mouth of River Cart

The Black Cart and White Cart rivers meet three-quarters of a mile upstream at Inchinnan where the White Cart is spanned by an opening cantilever bridge built in 1921. The White Cart flows through Paisley which despite its inland location once itself had an active shipbuilding industry with up to six yards being in operation in the town. The last of these, Fleming & Ferguson, established in 1885, remained in business down to 1969. Like Simons Lobnitz its main output was dredgers, and it had a particular connection with Argentina, and a model of an Argentine dredger from this yard may be seen in Paisley Museum. Their ships often fitted out in the Pudzeoch at Renfrew.

Passenger services from Paisley commenced at an early date. The steamer *Prince of Orange*, built by James Munn at Greenock, made her way up the difficult and winding waters of the Cart in July 1815 to provide the first steamer service from Paisley. Large crowds turned out to witness this significant development in the life of this important Renfrewshire textile town. Paisley Harbour was enlarged and the opening celebrated in April 1891 by a fleet of steamers sailing from Paisley to Rothesay. Charter trips by the Clyde River Steamer Club in 1959 using the *Countess of Breadalbane* and in 1966 with the *Maid of Argyll* are the only recent passenger sailings. Coasters and puffers used the Cart Navigation until it was, for the most part, abandoned in the 1970s. The lower reaches are, however, still maintained by Mitsui Babcock Energy.

⚲ Mitsui Babcock Energy

Their berth at the works of this well known firm of boiler makers is used by J & A Gardner's coasters. Their predecessor company, Babcock Power, built *Waverley's* replacement boiler in 1980. F. T. Everard's coasters such as *Speciality* and *Selectivity* – take boiler parts from these works to other sites in the United Kingdom, although more recently these cargoes have been handled from King George V Dock.

⚭ Rothesay Dock

This dock was officially inaugurated on 25th April 1907. It is not directly named after the Bute town, but in honour of the then Prince of Wales (later King George V) whose premier Scottish title was Duke of Rothesay and who performed the opening ceremony having sailed down-river from Renfrew, appropriately enough on

South West Renfrew showing Rothesay Dock (right), John Brown's (middle) and Bowling in the distance. The River Cart is seen on the left.
Photo: Hunting Aerofilms Ltd.

board the Caledonian Steam Packet Company's paddle steamer *Duchess of Rothesay*, built at the nearby Clydebank yard of J. & G. Thomson. Rothesay Dock was designed as a general trade dock and ships from all over world unlikely to be seen further upriver could be found here. Mineral cargoes formed a large part of its business. In the late 1930s it was much used for the import of scrap iron, which was often carried from America in hulls laid up since 1918 and sent over here for breaking-up. Rothesay Dock's use for importing iron ore declined after the reconstruction of General Terminus Quay in 1957, although it still continued to be employed for the importation of specialist ores and consignments for smaller companies.

Today Rothesay Dock continues to deal with a wide range of products. A tank farm has been established by an importer and distributor of petroleum products and ship bunkering facilities are being provided here. A scrap metal exporter has a stockyard near the tidal basin, which can accommodate vessels of 25,000 tons. Elsewhere in the Dock facilities are provided for handling cargoes of sand and road salt.

Crowds on the *Duchess of Hamilton* (1932) at Rothesay Dock for the launch of the *Queen Elizabeth 2* on 20/9/1967.

⚓N John Brown Shipbuilding & Engineering Company

Famed as the builder of the Queens and undoubtedly the Clyde's most famous name. The yard was founded here in 1872 as J & G Thomson, by two brothers who had previously worked under Robert Napier. The Thomsons had earlier run a yard at Govan which had been purchased by the Clyde Navigation Trust when they wished to create the Govan Dry Docks. During their Govan period the Thomsons built one of the West Coast's most famous ships – the paddle steamer *Iona* of 1864. This strikingly handsome ship was in service on MacBrayne's summer routes until 1935.

The Thomsons more or less inherited the role as main builder for Cunard that Napier had once enjoyed. Between 1863 and 1883 of the twenty eight ships that were added to the Cunard fleet no less than twenty one came from Thomson's yards at Govan or Clydebank.

After the move to Clydebank the firm continued to produce fine vessels, such as the MacBrayne flagship *Columba* in 1878. This famous vessel maintained, during the summer months, the prestigious MacBrayne "Royal Route" to the West Highlands. As the Company's promotional literature pointed out:

"The Route has been called the ROYAL ROUTE ever since her late Majesty Queen Victoria traversed it in 1847. She thrice visited the Highlands and twice sailed on the Company's Steamers."

In the first years of this century *Columba* sailed from Bridge Wharf at 7.00 a.m. calling at Partick, Greenock, Gourock and Dunoon, and Innellan, reaching Rothesay by 10.15 and arriving at Ardrishaig at 12.40, having sailed the 90 miles from Glasgow, with 12 intermediate stops in 5 hours 40 minutes, a demanding timetable only achievable by swift and skilful berthing and priority going to this prestige sailing. Slightly later the departure time was changed to 7.11 a.m. and the call at Partick abandoned.

The Company's brochure claimed that *Columba's* top speed was 22 knots – a more realistic estimate however places her speed at 19 knots. Passengers then transferred to the Crinan Canal steamer *Linnet* and cruised on through the canal to pick up another steamer such as the *Chevalier* to carry them forward to Oban "the Charing Cross of the Highlands", from where connections by road, rail and sea were available to "all points North". The "Royal Route" was much used by affluent holiday-makers coming up from England for shooting and fishing holidays in Highland lodges and hotels. Rail connections via Craigendoran (with steamer services forward to Dunoon), Greenock and Gourock were offered for passengers on the various railway company's overnight sleeper

Columba (1878) – in 1936.

services from London. When Para Handy of the puffer *Vital Spark* allowed his imagination to run away with him it was of the "Royal Rowt" he dreamed, and he visualised his beloved puffer sailing in a very different trade:

> "She should be carrying nothing but gentry for passengers, or nice genteel luggage for the shooting-lodges. . . "

Quite how the *Vital Spark* would have matched up to the *Columba* is unclear. The MacBrayne's literature waxed lyrical over their pride and joy's facilities:

> The Breakfast and Dining Saloon is 8 feet high, well ventilated and meals are served at any time. The Dining Saloon (forward) for Steerage or Fore-Cabin Passengers is light and airy.

> The Ladies' and Gentlemen's Cabins are elegantly fitted-up and there is a Shampooing and Hair-dressing Establishment, with a supply of every toilet requisite.

> Near the main entrance to the Saloon are a Book-stall and a Fruit-stall for Cabin Passengers. Steerage Passengers are provided with a separate Book-stall, Fruit-stall, and Ladies' Cabin forward.

The *Columba* also boasted an on-board Post Office handling 110,000 letters a month. This entitled her to the prized ante-nominal letters R.M.S. – Royal Mail Steamer. J. J. Bell in *The Glory of Scotland* enthused about the morning sailing on the *Columba*:

> The hardship of rising at six on a summer morning may be mitigated by the excellent breakfast served in the saloon, which in not a few cases appears to promote a glow of conscious virtue, and the passage down the river is really worthwhile.

What has been called the best looking Clyde steamer, and certainly the fastest one of her day, the *Glen Sannox* of 1892, was also built at the Clydebank yard for the Glasgow and South Western Railway.

In 1897 the Thomson yard was taken over by the Sheffield steel-making firm of John Brown & Company. Although the yard became famed as a builder of great ocean liners and the largest warships its output continued to be varied and included many other ships for Clyde river service and a succession of fast cross Channel turbine steamers for the railway companies, among these latter could be mentioned the 1947 *Arnhem* and the 1950 *Amsterdam* for the British Railways Harwich to Hook of Holland service.

It is however the great Cunarders and the major warships like the *Hood* and *Vanguard* with which the glory of the John Brown

Glen Sannox (1892).

Glen Sannox (1892-1925) being broken up at Port Glasgow.

name will always be associated. The building of these giant ships was only possible this far up the narrow waters of the Clyde by the careful alignment of the building berths with the mouth of the River Cart on the opposite bank. The modernisation of the yard under its new owners soon paid dividends with the contract to build the *Lusitania*, which was launched at Clydebank in June 1906 and was the largest liner of her era. Cunard, her owners, had wanted a prestige ship to recapture their earlier dominance on the North Atlantic service from German rivals. The Admiralty had an interest in a ship which could be converted in time of war into an auxiliary cruiser, although in the event the *Lusitania* was never taken into Royal Navy service – probably because at 31,550 tons and 787 feet length she was just too big and too fuel greedy. The *Lusitania* was sunk by the German submarine U20 in May 1915 in an incident which still arouses controversy. German sources claimed she was carrying munitions and was thus a legitimate target, a claim strenuously denied by the British government. In any event the loss of her 1198 passengers and crew, including many US citizens, outraged the American public and helped move opinion there towards an interventionist stance in the First World War.

Lusitania was swiftly followed by the even larger and more splendid *Aquitania* of 1913 which entered Cunard service in May 1914. Wartime service as a troopship followed and after the war reinstatement as a luxury transatlantic liner. Trooping duties followed again during the Second War and this four funnelled giant's long life ended at the Faslane shipbreakers on the Gareloch, just twenty miles from her birthplace, in 1950. The *Aquitania* well illustrates the rapid development of the Atlantic liner. In 1855

Aquitania (1914) – "The Ship Beautiful".

when Napier's yard had launched the iron paddle steamer *Persia* for Cunard she was at 376 feet with 3,600 hp engines and measuring 3,300 tons the giant ship of her day. In the 1880s the Inman Line's *City of Paris*, built at Clydebank, was at the forefront of technology, a steel screw steamer measuring 528 feet, equipped with 18,000 hp compound engines and of 10,699 tons. The *Aquitania* dwarfed her predecessors at 901 feet, 47,000 tons and disposing of 60,000 hp in her turbine engines.

During the First World War the Admiralty ordered a new battle-cruiser from John Brown – she was launched as HMS *Hood* in August 1918, too late for service in that war. Between the Wars the "mighty *Hood*" was, justifiably, the pride of the Royal Navy. During the Second World War the *Hood* engaged the German battleship *Bismarck* and the cruiser *Prinz Eugen* on 24th May 1941 and her light armour plating proved no match for the modern guns of the German ship. One German shell penetrated to a high explosive magazine and *Hood* was destroyed in an instant, with the loss of all but three members of her 1419 strong crew.

Work started on a new Cunarder, contract number 534, in 1930 but, due to the Depression, work was suspended on her and most of Brown's labour force laid off in December 1931. There was great rejoicing when the order to resume work was given in April 1934 and her launch as *Queen Mary* on 26 September 1934 was one of

The *Queen Mary* aground temporarily at Dalmuir Bend.

Queen Elizabeth (1940).

A ticket for the launch of the *Queen Elizabeth*.

the Clyde's red-letter days. She entered service in 1936 and on the outbreak of war was taken over for trooping duties. One extract from her wartime log indicates the contribution to the war effort that this great ship made on her high speed crossings:

"New York to Gourock 16,683 souls aboard. New York 25 July 1943. Gourock 30 July 1943. 3,353 miles, 4 days, 20 hours, 42 minutes. 28.73 knots. The greatest number of human beings ever embarked on one vessel."

The *Mary's* younger sister-ship *Queen Elizabeth* was launched in 1938 and in February 1940 was sent, in great secrecy, to New York from where she sailed to Sydney to convert to a wartime trooping role. In 1946 she re-fitted at Southampton and Gourock for her designed role as a luxury transatlantic liner. The *Queen Elizabeth* continued on the Southampton–New York run until 1968 when the economics of transatlantic liner services became too difficult for her to remain in service. Various attempts were made to find uses for her and she moved to Hong Kong to become a floating university but was destroyed by fire in January 1971. *Queen Mary* came out of service in 1967, the jet aircraft having virtually destroyed the transatlantic passenger trade and the age of year-round transatlantic liner crossings. Clydebank's pride was sold to the City of Long Beach, California and was converted into a museum, hotel and conference centre.

During the Second World War John Brown's won a contract to build a new battleship, which was launched as HMS *Vanguard* on 30th November 1944, the last British battleship ever built, and one destined never to fire a shot in anger. She was broken up at Faslane after only fifteen years of service.

The construction of the Royal Yacht *Britannia* provided a post-war high point for John Brown's and Clydebank when she was launched by the Queen in 1953. In 1965 the yard launched the Swedish-America Line's flagship *Kungsholm*. This handsome ship was eventually to be bought by P & O and re-christened *Sea Princess*.

Cunard came back to the Clydebank yard for their 1967 liner *Queen Elizabeth 2*. She was in part planned as a replacement for the *Queen Mary* but with a major cruising role reflecting the changed circumstances on the North Atlantic. *QE2* was plagued with turbine problems when she entered service in 1969 and she had to come back to the Clyde for repairs. In 1982 she was one of the merchant ships requisitioned for service in the Falklands War and carried 3000 troops to the South Atlantic. After her return from active service she was re-engined, in the interests of economy, as a diesel motor vessel at a German yard in Bremerhaven.

QE2 continues to carry out a world-wide cruising programme for Cunard. The inherent strength of the ship and the quality of her Clydebuilt workmanship was fully tested in September 1995 when, in hurricane conditions off the American coast, she was hit by a freak wave. Her Captain, Ronald Warwick, estimated the wave at ninety-five feet in height and described it as easily the biggest he had seen in thirty-eight years at sea. QE2 hit the 400 yard long wall of water, juddered and passed through with only superficial damage. "It's a magnificent ship," commented Captain Warwick and indeed QE2 is magnificent though she must unfortunately be seen as the last of her kind. The last in that long and glorious line of Cunard liners built on the Clyde, a line which started with the first four Cunarders of 1840, *Acadia, Britannia, Caledonia, Britannia* and which runs on through such memorable ships as the *Lusitania* and the *Aquitania* to the two later *Queens*. Sadly there is little chance of a new Cunarder being built on the Clyde. John Brown's is no more. The yard was sold to the Texas oil firm, Marathon and then passed into the ownership of the French controlled company UIE Shipbuilding (Scotland) Ltd. and is now engaged in the production of oil rigs and modules for the North Sea oil and gas industry. While these rigs may lack the romance of the *Queens* or the grandeur of a great battleship, they are, however, structures of epic size; indeed the company's largest rig to leave Clyde only managed to pass under the Erskine Bridge with 3" to spare and finishing work to rigs is often carried out in the wider areas of the river downstream.

Ñ Post Office Cable Wharf

This wharf was formerly used by cable laying ships. It closed in the 1960s and has now been filled in. When the new cable ship *Alert* was built at Fairfield in the 1960s this wharf was found to be too small and *Alert* had to lie at Rothesay Dock.

Ñ William Beardmore & Company

The origins of this famous company were to be found in the East End of Glasgow at Parkhead Forge. William Beardmore took over his father's forge in 1879 and developed it for the manufacture of guns and armour plate. He later diversified into shipbuilding, taking over what had been the Govan East yard of Robert Napier & Sons. Beardmore merged his business with Vickers Sons & Maxim, the world's largest private armaments manufacturer.

Beardmore moved his yard to a new site at Dalmuir where he could lay out a modern plant capable of tendering for the largest Admiralty contracts, and with the armour plate and gun making capacity available in his Glasgow forges offer an integrated warship construction facility. The Dalmuir yard, when completed in 1907 at a cost of £923,000, covered 90 acres and included a 5½ acre engine and boiler shop and a 7½ acre fitting out basin. Beardmore's development of the Dalmuir yard coincided with the growth of naval rivalry with Germany, the development of the heavily gunned *Dreadnought* class of battleships and the very active Admiralty building programme in the decade before the outbreak of war in 1914. Beardmore's fully shared in this pre-war building boom with four battleships being ordered in addition to three cruisers and two destroyers. During the First World War the Beardmore complex produced all manner of warships, munitions, aeroplanes, airships, etc. However the yard, although busy, never quite reached its capacity in the production of major warships for which it had been specially designed and expensively equipped.

After the war the yard attempted to diversify into merchant shipbuilding but was severely affected by the post-war recession. The international treaty limiting the number and size of capital ships – the Washington Naval Treaty of November 1921 – resulted in the Admiralty cancelling four battle cruiser orders. Three of these

Anchor Line's *Cameronia*, launched at Dalmuir by Beardmore's, 23/12/1919.

"super *Hoods*" had been earmarked for the Clyde, for Fairfield, John Brown and Beardmore. The yard was forced to scrabble around for other contracts and ended up in the uneconomical position of building small ships on its huge berths designed for building battleships. In 1930 the inevitable happened and what had been perhaps finest and most modern yard on the Clyde closed. In all 170 ships were built by Beardmore's at their Govan and Dalmuir yards. The company was also responsible, at its Inchinnan works in Renfrewshire, for building the R34 airship – the first airship to make a double crossing of the Atlantic. The Dalmuir yard site and fitting-out basin was partly taken over by Arnott Young.

The Beardmore name has not, however, totally vanished from the map. William Beardmore, who was created Lord Invernairn in 1921, was a noted sponsor of Antarctic exploration and the 200 mile long Beardmore Glacier in South Victoria Land was named in his honour by Sir Ernest Shackleton.

Arnott Young Shipbreakers

When Beardmore's yard closed part of the site was taken over as a shipbreaking concern, and many famous Clyde steamers were to end their lives here including the *Columba* and *Iona* in 1936.

Caledonia (1934) at Dalmuir Basin, 1970.

Caledonia of 1934 was laid up here before moving to the Thames in 1971. The shipbreaking concern has now closed and the site was redeveloped in the 1990s to form a private hospital run by Health Care International.

R Newshot Island

The remains of burnt vessels, damaged in the Kingston Dock fire of 1914, may still be seen at low water. Newshot Island is technically no longer an island since the Southern channel was allowed to silt up.

R Dalmuir Bend

The Cunarder *Queen Mary* ran aground here when going down river in March 1936 but was floated off on the rising tide without damage, thanks to the assistance of her attendant tugs.

N Dalmuir Sewage Works

A berth here is used by the sewage sludge vessels *Dalmarnock* and *Garroch Head*.

T. S. S. *Dalmarnock* (1925).

N Old Kilpatrick Oil Jetty

The jetty closed in 1980. The oil terminal here had been built for the Admiralty in 1918 and as oil fuel increasingly took over from coal a second terminal was later built on reclaimed land at Dunglass down river. In 1948 two jetties were in use and refined products were subsequently distributed from here. The steam lighter *Invertest* was often seen bunkering vessels on the river and carried this function out as far up river as the Broomielaw. The *Invertest* was also to be seen in John Brown's basin bunkering newly completed ships. *Waverley* and the Royal Fleet Auxiliary tanker *Pearleaf* had a special rendezvous at Old Kilpatrick oil jetty in August 1980 when *Pearleaf* carried out the last operational visit to the Admiralty Jetty.

R Erskine Bridge

This toll bridge was opened 1971 by Princess Anne, replacing a chain driven steam powered ferry. When the ferry ceased operations the redundant vessel was used as relief on the Renfrew Ferry route. The old chain house on the South Bank, which is now a private home, can still be seen from the river. A high-level bridge at Erskine was first proposed in 1934 – progress sometimes takes a little time! Long before the steam powered ferry came into service the Erskine crossing had been in use as a traditional cross-river route – the minister of Old Kilpatrick, on the Dumbartonshire side of the river, wrote in 1792:

> The ferry of Erskine, almost opposite to the church, is the communication for foot passengers, horses and carriages, across the river in this part of the country.

The Clyde can sometimes be seen as a barrier to communications – needing ferries, bridges and tunnels to allow the communities on either side of the river to keep in touch. However the Clyde's role as an important unifying force, as a corridor at the heart of a major region, as a means of communication and as a focus for the identity of the area, its character and culture, should not be over-looked. The phrase "Clyde Built" has always had an association with quality, and with the Clydesiders' pride in the work and life of their river. The agencies, such as local authorities, statutory bodies and voluntary organisations, some sixty in number, concerned with the development and management of the Clyde Estuary have united to form the Clyde Estuary Forum – a body whose aims are:

> to harness the economic and environmental advantages of the Clyde Estuary
>
> to bring about a regeneration of its role as a focus of activity
>
> to co-ordinate and manage this change on sustainable environmental principles and thereby
>
> to balance the commercial and environmental interests of the users of the estuary.

It is hoped to achieve these aims by producing a set of voluntary management guidelines which all interested parties will observe.

Boarding the *Erskine Ferry* at Old Kilpatrick in 1966.

Waverley sailing under the newly opened Erskine Bridge in 1971.

R̰ Bowling Bend

One of the awkward spots for navigation on the river. In the times before the introduction of radio a series of hailing stations were established at key points on the river. These were trellis-like erections where a man with a loudhailer advised ships of known traffic movements on the river. The hailing stations were to be found at Queen's Dock, Govan Pier and here at Bowling. With the development of radio this system was replaced by messages from Clydeport Estuary Control.

N̂ Entrance to Forth & Clyde Canal

The "Great Canal" was built between 1768 and 1790 and carried traffic the thirty five miles between here and Grangemouth with a three and a half mile extension into Port Dundas in Glasgow. The Canal basin is now used for laying-up small vessels although it is now substantially silted up and filled with many wrecked and abandoned vessels. The eighteenth century Custom's House, adjacent to the disused railway swing bridge, serves as a reminder of the significant part that Bowling played in international trade when the Canal first opened. At that time it was the main cargo route into the city and across to the East Coast. Many of the characteristic puffers which carried general cargoes around the Clyde estuary and Hebrides were built at yards on the Forth and Clyde Canal, at Maryhill, and most famously at the Kirkintilloch yard of J. & J. Hay Ltd.

N̂ Bowling Harbour

At one time Bowling was locally famous for being able to demonstrate five different modes of transport running side by side: river, canal, railway, road and tramway. Up to 1952 Bowling Harbour was the traditional winter lay-up base for those elements of the Clyde steamer fleet which were not required to carry out year-round services. Neil Munro, writing of this custom in his *Glasgow Evening News* column, observed:

It is the closing trip of the season; on Monday the steamer goes to sleep in Bowling; the shores of the Firth will see her no more till April. . . Summer steamers are bound to run shuddering into Bowling harbour for their winter berths when the snow is on the hills, and already it is white on Cruachan, Ben Buidhe, and Ben Ime – . . .

Preparing for summer in Bowling Harbour, *Eagle III* and *Isle of Arran*.

Ⓢ Erskine Hospital

Erskine House was built in 1828 for Lord Blantyre to designs by Sir Robert Smirke, the architect of the British Museum in London. During the First World War it was converted into The Princess Louise Scottish Hospital for Limbless Sailors and Soldiers. The hospital was opened by Princess Louise, Duchess of Argyll, who sailed, from her home at Rosneath Castle, to Erskine in what had once been Clutha No. 4 but had been converted to a yacht by the Clyde Navigation Trust and now bore the historic name *Comet*. Erskine Hospital continues in its role of caring for ex-servicemen and women injured in the wars and conflicts of this century.

N̂ Scott & Sons, Bowling

A yard was established here by a member of the distinguished Greenock shipbuilding family of Scott in 1851. The yard specialised in the production of smaller vessels such as puffers, coasters, tugs etc. Among these little ships may be included the *Minard* (1926) and the *Ardyne* (1928) for Clyde Cargo Steamers Ltd. The Scott family owned the pleasure cruiser *Carola* which has now been presented to Scottish Maritime Museum at Irvine. Formerly on the South Coast she was sailed to Irvine via the

Caledonian Canal. The yard now concentrates on the repair and maintenance of small craft such as the Renfrew ferries.

↑ Dunglass Castle

Dunglass Castle was built, in the fourteenth century, as a stronghold of the chiefs of the Clan Colquhoun. The building was added to in the sixteenth century but later the stones were robbed to repair the quay at Dunglass. A mansion house was built in the nineteenth century. Within the grounds is one of three local monuments to Henry Bell of *Comet* fame, an obelisk erected in 1839, nine years after his death. Other monuments to Bell are to be seen in Helensburgh and over his grave in Rhu Churchyard.

≈ Lang Dyke

This structure was built in 1773 as part of a plan to deepen the river. The Clyde was historically a shallow and winding river with many sand banks and other hazards to navigation. Glasgow was anxious to be able to play a full part in trade but as late as the eighteenth century the river was impassable for anything but the smallest of ships. A port was developed at Newark, now Port Glasgow, down river on the Renfrewshire shore, but this was not seen as an ideal solution as there was still the need to split and transfer loads with all the cost and risks of damage that this employed. After the Union of 1707 Glasgow gradually developed a large trade with the American and West Indian colonies and the influential Glasgow "Tobacco Lords" were continually pressing the City Council to take steps to improve the Clyde navigation.

Various engineers were consulted who proposed canalising the river. However in 1768 the English engineer John Golborne came up with a more ingenious plan which would, in effect, make the Clyde deepen itself. Some dredging would be done but short dykes at right angles to the banks would be built to speed up the flow of water, and thus to increase the scouring effect of the river. This, it was hoped, would allow a four or five foot deep channel to be created all the way up to Glasgow.

Golborne's contract centred on making Dumbuck Ford, one of the worst bottlenecks on the river, 6' deep and with a 300' wide navigable channel at low water. For the successful accomplishment of this work he was to receive the sum of £2300. In 1775 the City Council granted him an additional £1500 and a silver cup for his efforts in deepening the ford by ten inches more than the contract had called for.

By 1773 coasting vessels were able to unload Irish oatmeal at the Broomielaw – but with only four feet of water the river was still only practicable for very small vessels. The Lang Dyke was built parallel to the flow of the river to scour away a particularly bad shoal area at this point.

The next phase in the deepening of the river came in 1806 when the great engineer Thomas Telford was consulted and he recommended joining up the ends of Golborne's projecting dykes, or groynes as they were called, and work on this was virtually complete by 1812. Traffic on the river was, however, still limited. When the *Comet* made her first trip down-river, even though she only drew four feet, she still managed to ground on a sandbank at Renfrew despite Bell planning her time of departure from the Broomielaw to avoid low water. Fortunately the *Comet* was so small that the crew could simply step over the side and push the little steamer off the sand bank.

The first efforts at dredging were carried out from the river banks using large rakes or "porcupine ploughs" which were worked by hand-powered capstans. The eighteenth century travel writer and naturalist Thomas Pennant gives a good description of the process as he witnessed it in operation on the Clyde in June 1772:

> After breakfast, survey the machines for deepening the river which were then at work: they are called ploughs, are large hollow cases, the back is of cast iron, the two ends of wood; the other side open. These are drawn across the river by means of capstans. . . which scrapes the bottom, and brings up at every return half a ton of gravel. . . Thus twelve hundred tons are cleared every day.

Obviously this method only worked efficiently on the narrower stretches of the river but it and the scouring process were effective enough to ensure that by 1818 foreign-going ships were able to sail directly to the Broomielaw. By 1824 steam-powered dredgers were at work deepening the river and widening and straightening the channel. Even before the development of this application of steam power hand and horse powered bucket dredgers had been used.

The process of deepening the river continued, although not without set-backs and problems. Sometimes the deepening itself caused some of the difficulties. In 1854, for example, once the Blawarthill Sandbank had been removed an underlying vein of rock 925' long by 320' wide was discovered – and discovered in the most painful fashion by the *Glasgow* steamship running onto the rock when outward bound, heavily laden for New York. Fifteen years were spent boring and blasting away at what became known as the Elderslie Rock and 110,000 tons of whinstone and boulder clay had to be removed to produce the desired uniform 20' depth at low water.

N Dunglass Oil Jetty

This jetty was used for bunkering by many of the river steamers. *Clyde Venturer* and *Clyde Enterprise*, then the *Borrowdale H*, a converted trawler, took bunkers to ships unable to come alongside. Now, with the loss of all the river's bunkering barges, ships on the river require to fuel from road tankers supplied at Rothesay Dock.

N Dumbuck Quarry

Dumbuck Hill, the site of a prehistoric vitrified fort, is a landmark on the Dunbartonshire shore, although a landmark which is steadily being eaten away by quarrying. The Dumbuck area has yielded fascinating evidence of the early dwellers on the Clyde. A crannog, or artificial island dwelling, was found in the Clyde off Dumbuck in 1895 and among the many artefacts recovered from the investigation of the site was a dug-out canoe – the first type of Clyde-built boat of which we have any evidence. The Dumbuck canoe was hollowed out from a thirty foot long trunk of an oak tree. Dredging operations on the Clyde have produced a number of other dug-out canoes in the Dunglass and Milton areas.

N Dumbarton

The maritime history of Dumbarton stretches back many centuries. It is often suggested that the Romans may have had a naval base here in connection with the Antonine Wall, which stretched from Bowling to the River Forth. Indeed Dumbarton Rock would seem an obvious strategic point to be used in this way although there is no written evidence to support such a claim and no archaeological evidence of Roman occupation has been found on the Rock. Dumbarton's first entry in the historical record is in the eighth century as "Alcluith" – the rock on the Clyde. It was, until the eleventh century, the capital of the independent British kingdom of Strathclyde – a powerful state whose territories ran from the head of Loch Lomond to Morecambe Bay in Lancashire. King Robert the Bruce, who had a manor house near Dumbarton, kept his great ship here in the 1320s. It was from Dumbarton Castle that the young Mary Queen of Scots left for France in 1547 and Dumbarton served as a naval base for the Scottish Kings in their on-going struggle to control the Hebridean and Highland chiefs. For example, in 1598 King James VI commanded all masters and owners of ships in Glasgow, Ayr, Irvine, Dumbarton and the other West coast towns to hold their vessels in readiness for his arrival in Dumbarton on 20th August when a choice would be made of their ships for the Royal expedition to Kintyre. In the event Robert Jamieson of Ayr was the lucky (or unlucky) man chosen to carry King James to Kintyre – while the other shipowners of Ayr were to lend:

> . . . the best and maist able marineris

and also to supply such artillery and munitions as they might have to Jamieson. Clearly a trip to Argyllshire in 1598 was no light matter!

Dumbarton was once an important international trading port. The burgh merchants' ships sailed to many parts of the British Isles and the continent. An entry dating from 1595 in the town's port book or register of ship entries, shows John Smollett, a burgess of Dumbarton, reporting his ship *Providence* as having arrived in the Clyde with 50 tuns of "hie country wines" laden at Bordeaux. Smollett was engaged in the traditional claret trade between the Gironde estuary and the appreciative and enthusiastic wine drinkers of Scotland. In 1610 the register shows a Dutch skipper arriving at Dumbarton with timber and marine stores including a hundred anchors, twenty four masts and fourteen score of fir spars. The register also gives details of many ships whose ports of origin were in France, Norway, England, Germany, Ireland and the Netherlands trading into Dumbarton in the seventeenth century. Apart from timber and naval stores from Scandinavia and the Baltic, and wine from France, one of the commonest cargoes was salt, usually imported from the Bay of Biscay. In the days before canning or refrigeration large quantities of salt were required for the process of preserving meat and fish for winter supplies and for use at sea.

In 1658 the City of Glasgow had proposed to Dumbarton that an out-port for Glasgow should be built here. The Dumbarton Town Council rejected this proposal on the somewhat narrow-minded grounds that:

> . . . the influx of mariners would tend to raise the prices of butter and eggs to the inhabitants.

The Glasgow proposal was perhaps never likely to be a popular one – there was a long history of rivalry between the two towns and feelings were running high. Glasgow had instructed her merchants to stop using Dumbarton as the official port of entry and to record their imports in the Glasgow Town Clerk's office instead. Dumbartonians went across to Newark and boarded ships berthed there belonging to Glasgow merchants and committed "many riots" – for which piece of unruly behaviour the burgh of Dumbarton was fined £500.

The yellow and black Leven buoy marks the entrance to the River Leven. The banks of the Leven have seen the rise and fall of dozens of shipbuilding companies over the centuries and witnessed the launch of several thousand ships. The great name in Dumbarton shipbuilding was that of William Denny & Brothers, who from the foundation of the firm in 1844 to their closure in 1963 built 1460 ships at their various yards in the town. Other members of the Denny dynasty had been building in Dumbarton from the early years of the nineteenth century and many other, often quite short-lived, companies also operated on the banks of the Leven. The earliest steamship to cross the English Channel – the *Margery* – was built in Dumbarton by John Denny in 1814. Other famous names in Dumbarton's early shipbuilding history include James Lang, who built the *Leven* steamer in 1821. The engine of this ship, one of the early works of Robert Napier, has been preserved and can still be inspected in Dumbarton.

Among the notable achievements of William Denny & Brothers' yard were the world's first commercial turbine steamer, the *King Edward* of 1901, and the world's first all-steel merchant ship, the *Rotomahana* of 1878. The company was also extremely advanced in having, from 1883, its own ship model experiment tank. Use of this tank to refine designs and hull shapes was largely instrumental in Denny Brothers becoming highly successful specialist builders of fast cross-channel steamers. For many years they, along with Fairfield and John Brown, dominated the English Channel with a succession of splendid ships built for the British and foreign railway and ferry companies. The ship model tank has been preserved and now operates as an out-station of the Irvine-based Scottish Maritime Museum.

William Denny & Brothers were the builders of Scotland's first all-welded vessel – the car ferry *Robert the Bruce* launched in 1934 for the Firth of Forth ferry service. This ship was also the first diesel-electric paddle vessel built in the United Kingdom. All this innovation was perhaps possible because the Denny company took over ownership of the Forth ferry service at Queensferry in 1932.

For home waters Denny built such well-known Clyde and West Coast steamers as the *Duchess of Argyll* in 1906, the *Glen Sannox* of 1925, the *King George V* of 1926, the 1930 turbine *Duchess of Montrose*, the 1933 *Queen Mary*, advertised as "Britain's finest pleasure steamer" and the 1934 paddle steamer *Caledonia*. Among the last ships to be launched from Denny's yard before its closure in 1963, was the 1961 ferry *Caledonian Princess* for the Stranraer-Larne service. This ship now lies at Anderston Quay, renamed *Tuxedo Princess*.

Duchess of Argyll (1906).

Caledonia (1934) launched at Dumbarton 1/2/1934.

Duchess of Montrose in Denny's Basin immediately after launch 10/5/1930.

One short-lived, and otherwise unremarkable, Dumbarton shipyard was that of Scott & Linton who in a three year tenancy of the famous Woodyard, on the West bank of the Leven, produced only nine ships before becoming bankrupt. However one of these nine ships is perhaps the most famous of all the classic sailing clippers – the glorious *Cutty Sark* launched in 1869. Scott and Linton's business failed while she was still on the stocks and the clipper had to be completed by William Denny. She was designed for the China tea trade, a route on which great premiums were available for the ships which could reach home first with the new season's crop, hence the emphasis on fine lines, large sail areas and high speeds. In fact most of the *Cutty Sark's* great feats were to come in the Australian wool trade. After an eventful and varied career she is now preserved at Greenwich as an evocative reminder of the great days of sail. Two events contemporary with her launch signalled the beginning of the end for the great clipper ships – the opening of the Suez canal in 1869 cut weeks off the previous round the Cape route to the Far East and Australasia and, combined with the development, by John Elder, of the compound engine with its greater fuel economy, opened up these long-distance routes to the steam ship.

Dumbarton's second largest shipyard was the long established firm of Archibald MacMillan & Son. This firm occupied the Churchyard site in the centre of the town between 1834 and 1930. The giant Hiram Walker Distillery, a conspicuous red-brick building on the Leven opened in 1938, marks the spot where this famous yard once stood. In the Depression of the 1920s and 30s there was enormous over-capacity in the shipbuilding industry and moves toward the merger and consolidation of shipbuilding yards. The Harland & Wolff group took over various yards on the river, including MacMillan's. However much rationalisation and merging took place in these company manoeuvrings it still left the overall capacity with the same number of yards chasing ever fewer orders. The idea emerged among shipbuilders of creating a body which would buy up redundant shipyards and "sterilise" them by taking them permanently out of production. This body, National Shipbuilders Security Ltd., had financial support from the Government and benefited from a levy on operational shipbuilders and also took the proceeds from the sale of yards. This was a drastic way to cure the overcapacity and the company's operations inevitably caused much unrest and disharmony. Among the major Clyde yards which were completely taken out of production by National Shipbuilders Security Ltd were Beardmore, Napier & Miller, D. & W. Henderson, Caird of Greenock and, just four years short of its centenary and after launching 500 ships, Archibald MacMillan & Son.

In Dumbarton, as in all the other shipbuilding centres on the river, the shipyards were the most obvious and perhaps most glamorous manifestations of the industry. However behind the romance of the yards, their cranes and slipways and the emotion of launch days there lay a huge supporting cast of other industries. Engine works, foundries, rope-works, boat-yards to build life-boats and work boats, and a dozen other related concerns were all involved in the making of ships great and small. Even within a single shipyard the range of trades and skills involved was bewilderingly large. Yards, like Denny's, which concentrated on passenger vessels employed large numbers of workers in the decorative departments. These departments were among the few areas of the shipbuilding industry to employ women workers in peacetime – although some women and girls were employed as tracers in the drawing office and during the crisis of war women were suddenly found able to carry out many of the tasks which had previously been reserved for men.

Dumbarton, like most self-respecting Clyde towns, once had its own steamer pier. From the first days of the Clyde steamers in the early nineteenth century there had been calls by down-river steamers to Dumbarton Quay in the centre of the town. Dumbarton indeed had its own local steamer company which ran services from Dumbarton into Glasgow from as early as 1815. These services, both the Glasgow based and the Dumbarton based ones, had declined after the railway had come to Dumbarton in 1858. In any case the Quay was quite a long way off the main down-river steamer track and passengers to other destinations doubtless resented the diversion and delay involved in calling in to Dumbarton. In any event, a possibly over-enthusiastic Provost and Town Council built a new pier jutting out from the Castle Rock into the main channel of the Clyde and this was opened with great celebrations, including a salvo of gunfire from the Castle, in 1874. Unfortunately the pier, although certainly more convenient for Clyde traffic, was a very long walk from the centre of the town and most Dumbartonians wanting to travel down river took the train to Craigendoran or Helensburgh and the new pier proved something of a white elephant.

In the constricted waters of the Clyde it is not surprising that accidents and collisions occur. Even at Dumbarton, where the river widens out, the navigable channel is still quite narrow, and good traffic management is required. One of the more notable collisions on the Clyde took place off Dumbarton on the evening of the 25th May 1923 between the Hogarth steamer *Baron Vernon* and the

Baron Vernon (1922) sunk following a collision with the *Metagama*, May 1923.

Canadian Pacific Railways emigrant ship *Metagama*. The *Metagama* was outward bound for Quebec and Montreal from Prince's Dock with one thousand passengers on board. She had been advised that the river was clear and was still being assisted by tugs when she collided with the *Baron Vernon*, inward bound from Italy with a cargo of ore and esparto grass. The much smaller *Baron Vernon* was seriously holed below the water line and her captain, to minimise danger and avoid any chance of blocking the channel ran her aground on the North side of the river. The *Metagama* was also damaged, but much less seriously and returned to Prince's Dock for repairs but was able to leave for Canada four days later. The *Baron Vernon*, despite attempts to lighten her by off-loading her cargo, proved to be stuck fast on her sandbank and after a month the Clyde Navigation Trust gave up hope of her being towed off, and advertised for salvage companies to get rid of what was a potential hazard to traffic on the river. The unfortunate *Baron Vernon* was just a year out of her West Hartlepool builder's yard when the accident happened and she had been regularly trading between Glasgow and Spanish and Mediterranean ports. In November 1924 the Clyde Navigation Trust agreed to present the Hogarth Line with a bill for £41,392 – the cost of removing the *Baron Vernon* from the river. It was raised on 23 July 1924.

The *Metagama* was a Clyde-built ship, the product of Barclay Curle's yard at Scotstoun. Launched in 1914, she had acquired a reputation as a "bride's ship" from the number of emigrant brides to be who went out to North America on her after the First World War. Immediately prior to the trip on which she collided with the *Baron Vernon*, her last voyage to Canada had been a special, and highly publicised, sailing from Stornoway in which several hundred people from Lewis had emigrated en masse. A year after her Clyde accident she was to be involved in another collision, leading to her stranding, on the coast of Newfoundland.

Finlaystone House

The old house of Finlaystone is now largely hidden in the late nineteenth century reconstruction undertaken by the Glasgow architect J. J. Burnet. The mansion house was owned by the Earls of Glencairn – the fifth Earl was prominent in the early history of the Scottish Reformation and John Knox is said to have celebrated Communion here in 1556. The estate, with its gardens and woods, is now open to the public with a visitor centre and ranger service.

§ Timber Ponds

These used to stretch along the South bank of the Clyde between Langbank and Port Glasgow. Timber was seasoned by floating in these pond areas and was contained by a row of stakes driven into the river bed.

§ Port Glasgow

Newark had long been a location on the Clyde where ships could load and unload. In 1655 Thomas Tucker, an Excise Officer of the Cromwellian Government, reported that Newark was:

> . . . a small place where there are (besides the laird's house of the place) some four or five houses, but before them a pretty good roade, where all vessels doe ride, unlade, and send theyr goods up the river to Glasgowe in small boats. . .

In 1662 Glasgow City Council purchased thirteen acres of land at Newark to create a deep-water port for the City – previously the city's shipping trade had largely been carried out through ports on the Ayrshire coast. The new location in Renfrewshire was much more convenient and the trade of what became known as Port Glasgow swiftly increased. The main Custom House for the Clyde was established here in 1710 and James Watt designed a graving-dock for Port Glasgow in 1762. The trading patterns of the Glasgow merchants, whose ships sailed out from Port Glasgow to the Americas and the West Indies, are suggested by the motto on the coat of arms of Port Glasgow:

> Ter et quater anno revisens aequor Atlanticum impune – Three and four times a year revisiting the Atlantic with impunity.

Port Glasgow was to become one of the great centres of the early steamship building. The yard of John & Charles Wood launched many of the early Clyde steamers, including the *Comet*. Indeed of the first twenty steam-boats to ply on the Clyde nine came from this yard and a further three from other Port Glasgow builders. The Woods' yard also built the first Cunarder, *Acadia*, in 1840 on sub-contract from Robert Napier. John Wood was described by the great Victorian naval architect John Scott Russell as:

> . . . a diligent, accomplished and scientific constructor. . . a consummate artist in shipbuilding

and his excellence in wooden ship-building was widely recognised.

L'Atlantique (1931) arriving off Greenock with Dutch tugs *Ganges, Wittezee, Nordzee* and *Indus* on 13/3/1936. The 41,000 ton, fire-damaged vessel was being taken to Port Glasgow for scrap but to ensure that she did not impede the passage of the new *Queen Mary*, she was moored well clear of the channel until the Cunarder had passed down-river on 24/3/1936.

The *L'Atlantique* (1931), with Steele-Bennie tugs *Campaigner, Warrior Chieftain* and *Wrestler,* arriving for scrap at Smith & houston, Port Glasgow. It took ten tugs to beach her.

Among many other, now vanished, yards in the Port Glasgow area were Murdoch & Murray, Robert Duncan & Company, Russell & Company, Dunlop Bremner & Company Ltd., Clyde Shipbuilding & Engineering Company and William Hamilton & Company Ltd. A listing of this last company's work on hand in 1912 suggests something of the activity and range of contracts of an average Clyde yard at this time:

> Floating Dock for H.M. Navy; passenger steamer for La Compania Mexicana de Navigacion, Vera Cruz; passenger and cargo steamer for Grace Brothers, London; two cargo steamers for Stoomvaart Maatschippij Nederland of Amsterdam; cargo steamer for Rankin, Gilmour & Company, Liverpool; passenger and cargo steamer for New York and South America Line, New York; steamer for Lamport & Holt, Liverpool; and steamer for Koninklyke West-Indische Maildienst, Amsterdam.

Truly in that age the Clyde built for the world.

Lamont's Yard at Port Glasgow, the successor to the Clyde Shipbuilding and Engineering Company mentioned above, at their now closed Castle Yard, built the current Clyde car ferries *Jupiter* and *Juno* in 1973 and 1974. The yard's fitting-out pier remains, otherwise all traces of this yard have been swallowed up by the A8 Port Glasgow by-pass.

Car ferry *Juno* on the stocks at Lamont's, 1974.

Newark Castle (the "laird's house" of Tucker's report) – which dates in part from 1484 – makes an impressive sight from the river. Most of the castle dates from the end of the sixteenth century when the Maxwell family extended it. The industrialisation and growth of Port Glasgow around this well preserved relic perhaps slightly detracts from its impact but it remains a splendid example of a Scottish fortified mansion house. It is now in the care of Historic Scotland.

Ferguson's Shipyard

The last surviving shipyard in the Port Glasgow and Greenock area. Among its recent output was the new Caledonian MacBrayne ferry *Isle of Lewis* for the Ullapool-Stornoway service. In 1984 they launched the car ferry *Isle of Arran*. The lighthouse tender *Pharos*, based at Oban, is another product of this yard which may be seen in Scottish waters. The *Lord of the Isles* was also built here for Caledonian MacBrayne's mail and car ferry service to Coll, Tiree and the Outer Isles. She entered service in 1989. Recently three vessels, *Red Osprey, Red Eagle* and *Red Falcon*, for Red Funnel, Isle of Wight service were built here.

Lithgow's Shipyard

A complex group of yards in Port Glasgow, after many changes of ownership, came together in 1918 as Lithgow's Ltd and became one of the best known names on the river. The Lithgow family involvement in the management of shipbuilding here dates from 1874 when W. T. Lithgow became a partner in Russell & Company's yard. Lithgow's highly productive yards produced over 1.2 million tons of shipping during the Second World War. During part of the War the English artist Stanley Spencer was engaged as an official war artist to record life and work in Lithgow's yard and his large scale paintings from this period give a vivid impression of the wartime Clyde. In 1969 Lithgow's merged with Scott's of Greenock to form Scott Lithgow Ltd. In the 1960s and 1970s the Port Glasgow yard built extensively for Scottish Ship Management, the Lyle Shipping Company. They also were noted for the construction of super-tankers such as the *World Endeavour* and *World Score*. Because of the yard's restrictions on size these were built together in halves and joined down river in the Firth of Clyde Dry Dock. A prominent landmark on the Port Glasgow waterfront is the 270 ton lift Arrol Crane installed at this yard.

§ Comet Replica

A full size replica of the Clyde's first steamship the *Comet*, built in 1962 for the 150th anniversary of the first commercial steamship sailing, can be seen next to the main road running through Port Glasgow. This replica sailed on the original route to Helensburgh as part of the anniversary celebrations.

Comet replica (1962) at Bridge Wharf.

Ticket for a special sailing by *Countess of Breadalbane*.

§ Great Harbour – Greenock

This is now used by the vessels of the Royal Naval Auxiliary Service. The Great Harbour was formed in the 1880s by building a massive river wall from Garvel Point to Inchgreen. The effect of this was to create and enclose a large tidal basin. The Great Harbour was the first public undertaking in Scotland in the course of the construction of which electric lighting was used.

§ James Watt Dock – Greenock

Formerly much used for the importation of sugar cane for the Tate & Lyle refinery, James Watt Dock is now closed to all but Caledonian MacBrayne ferries and for the final painting and finishing works on ships which have had a refit at Garvel Dry Dock.

It is used by the Fishery Protection Fleet and was used, until 1981, by the vessels of the Ocean weather service.

It was in this dock in 1974-75 that *Waverley* was restored to her original L.N.E.R. colours with the black, white and red funnels, having been sold for the legendary pound by Caledonian MacBrayne Ltd.

Adjacent to the Dock is "Siberia Point" so nicknamed from its exposure to the coldest winter winds. George Brown & Company had a small shipyard here between 1900 and 1983 which specialised in the production of coasting vessels, tugs and fishing boats.

Clansman and *Waverley* in James Watt Dock, 1975.

§ Garvel Dry Dock

A new company formed from the former Lamont Dry Dock further down river in East India Harbour. When the Lamont company closed in the late 1980s some workers re-opened the old Garvel Dry Dock – one of only two operational dry docks left in the Firth of Clyde, the other being at Troon on the Ayrshire coast. The Garvel Dry Dock is the only dock able to accommodate the 57 foot wide *Waverley* which often has her pre-season inspection and painting done here.

§ Scott's of Greenock

The complex of yards which lay between James Watt Dock and Victoria Harbour has a very good claim to be considered as the cradle of Clyde shipbuilding. What was, until its closure, the oldest continuous shipbuilding concern on the Clyde was centred here. From 1711 until its merger in 1969 with Lithgow's of Port Glasgow the Scott family built some 900 ships in their Cartsburn and Cartsdyke yards. The firm started with the construction of small sailing smacks and took part in every technical development, from the introduction of steam, to the move to iron and steel construction. They also built extensively for the Royal Navy. Scott's yard indeed built the first of the new *Dreadnought* battleships to be allocated to a Clyde yard – HMS *Colossus* – which was laid down in July 1909. The Greenock yard was also to develop a particular specialisation in submarine construction.

Like the other specialist warship builders such as Fairfield and John Brown, Scott's yard formed part of the technical elite of the Clyde industry and were able to combine warship building with the highest class of merchant work. There were many similarities in scale and engineering equipment between a battleship and a crack ocean liner – and yards like John Brown's could efficiently turn out both. Equally there were obvious similarities between a fast cross-channel ferry or turbine pleasure steamer and a destroyer or sloop – and yards like William Denny's specialised in both.

Scott's yard built many ships for Alfred Holt and Company, including, in 1865, the three ships with which Holt started their service to China – the *Ajax*, *Agamemnon* and *Achilles*. Incorporated in the Scott's complex from 1966 was the Greenock Dockyard Company – which had built many ships for the Clan Line.

Like many Clyde yards there was a close connection between shipbuilders and shipowners. Sometimes this started with builders being partly paid for their work in shipping company shares but as the years went on many of the yards became substantial shareholders in shipping companies and in other cases, as with Greenock Dockyard, shipping companies owned or had major interests in yards. From the 1940s Greenock Dockyard had become a wholly owned subsidiary of Clan Line Steamers Ltd. Among other well known examples of inter-locking directorships between yards and shipowners was William Denny & Bros. of Dumbarton's link with the Irrawaddy Flotilla Company and Paddy Henderson.

Victoria Harbour – Greenock

This is the base for the present fleet of Cory Ship Towage tugs and also for the buoy tender *Torch*. *Waverley* was engined in Victoria Harbour by Rankine & Blackmore's Eagle Foundry .

East India Harbour – Greenock

Work started on the building of East India Harbour in 1805 and it was completed in 1809. The Harbour is the work of the distinguished Scottish engineer John Rennie. It is now used only by pleasure craft. After the closure of Bowling Harbour in 1952 East India Harbour was used by some of the Clyde river and Highland steamers for their winter lay-up. East India Harbour closed to commercial traffic in the 1980s. One part of the harbour was traditionally known as the Bristol Berth from its use by Bristol Channel steamers.

P.S. *Waverley* (1947) at Victoria Harbour in 1947.

As the name "East India" suggests Greenock had a large overseas trade; a trade not confined to the East Indies – Greenock developed during the eighteenth century as a major port of entry for products from North and Central America and the Caribbean – timber, tobacco and above all sugar. Thomas Tucker in 1655 noted that Greenock's maritime trade then consisted of:

> . . . seamen or fishermen tradeing for Irelande or the isles in open boates . . .

and went on to describe the limited port facilities of the town:

> . . .there is a mole or peere, where vessels in stresse of weather may ride, and shelter themselves before they pass up to Newarke . . .

By the end of the seventeenth century Greenock shipping had developed beyond "tradeing for Irelande" and indeed one of the ships of the ill-fated Darien Expedition in 1696 – the plan to establish a Scottish trading colony in Central America – was fitted out at Greenock. The development of trade across the Atlantic from the Clyde in the eighteenth century explains much of the prosperity of Glasgow and the Clyde towns in this period and their enthusiasm for schemes of dock building and river improvements. In Walter Scott's *Rob Roy* the Glasgow merchant, Bailie Nicol Jarvie, expresses his view on the benefits the Union of 1707 had brought to the West of Scotland:

> Now, since St. Mungo catched herrings in the Clyde, what was ever like to gar us flourish like the sugar and tobacco-trade. Will ony body tell me that, and grumble at the treaty that opened us up a road west-awa' yonder?

The trade of the town greatly increased, only being checked by the American War of Independence (1775-1783). After the end of the War the boom returned with a tripling in Greenock's trade between 1784 and 1791.

The Bailie's reference to catching herring in the Clyde serves as a reminder that Greenock, before its rise to fame as a shipbuilding and engineering centre and as a great trading port, was famed for its herring fisheries, with around 150 fishing boats sailing out of the town in the seventeenth and eighteenth centuries. Greenock's dependence on the herring was indicated by the burgh's older motto:

> Let herrings swim that trade maintain

This splendidly specific sentiment was changed around 1830 for the more generally applicable:

God speed Greenock

Another view on the former importance of Greenock as a centre of trade comes from the English novelist Daniel Defoe who made a tour in Scotland in the 1720's and wrote of Greenock:

. . .tis not an ancient place, but seems to be grown up in later years, only by being a good road for ships, and where the ships ride that come into, and go out from Glasgow, just as the ships for London do in the downs. It has a castle to command the road and the town is well built, and has many rich trading families in it. It is the chief town on the West of Scotland for the herring fishing; and the merchants of Glasgow, who are concerned in the fishery, employ the Greenock vessels for the catching and curing the fish, and for several parts of their other trades, as well as carrying them afterwards abroad to market..

Their being ready on all hands to go to sea, makes the Glasgow merchants often leave their ships to the care of those Greenock men; and why not? for they are sensible they are their best seamen; they are also excellent pilots for those difficult seas.

It was not for nothing that a fine salt herring used to be popularly known as a "Glasgow Magistrate".

However local folklore suggests that not all visitors to Greenock were as impressed or as well received as Tucker and Defoe. During the Napoleonic Wars, so one version of the legend goes, a fishing boat put into Greenock harbour. On board was an ape which the owners had dressed in the uniform of a French soldier. This untoward sight so alarmed the citizens of Greenock that they promptly executed the unfortunate beast as a French spy – leading to a traditional taunt from the citizens of the rival town of Port Glasgow – "Who hung the monkey?"

Greenock was to retain a role as a major port – at the end of the nineteenth century it was ranked fourth in Britain, behind London, Liverpool and Glasgow, for the number and tonnage of coasting trade vessels discharging there.

Greenock played a full part in the story of emigration over the centuries and it is appropriate that the town has plans for a museum celebrating the world wide contribution and achievement of the Scots.

§ Custom House Quay

This area has now been redeveloped and the Custom House, built in 1818 at a cost of £30,000 to plans by the architect William Burn, is now a museum and the Quayside has been extensively rebuilt. Downriver from the Customs House is the James Watt College's watefront campus; and a new water/ice complex built by Inverclyde District Council at a cost of £17 million and offering a full range of facilities for sporting and recreational use of pools and ice rinks. A miniplex cinema is planned to open in 1996 to complete the redevelopment of the Quay area. Adjacent to Custom House Quay were the offices of tug companies Steel & Bennie and Cory. The clock tower was erected in 1868 and is a familiar waterfront landmark. Between 1988 and 1991 Custom House Quay was closed to the *Waverley*, although from 1975 to 1987 and since it re-opened in 1992 it has proved an excellent pick up point for her and is now a regular call on her cruising programme.

§ Caird & Company, Westburn Yard

This remarkable yard, tucked in between the East India Harbour and the Albert Harbour was intimately linked with the Peninsular & Oriental Steam Navigation Company, normally building two ships for them each year, although a 1912 listing shows that sometimes even more work could be on hand, as in that year no fewer than five P & O vessels were building. In 1916 the firm was sold to Harland & Wolff and it was closed down as part of the rationalisations in shipbuilding in 1928.

§ Albert Harbour

Albert Harbour was built between 1862 and 1867. It was used by many Clyde and coastal steamers for their winter lay-up. It closed in 1967 and the site was redeveloped as a new ocean terminal. Adjacent to Albert Harbour was Princes Pier, the steamer terminal for the Glasgow & South Western Railway Company based at Glasgow's St. Enoch Station. The pier was originally opened in 1866. The fierce rivalry between the competing railway companies played a large part in the development of their steamer terminals. Competition from the Caledonian Railway, which had leapfrogged Greenock and run a rail line down to a new terminal at Gourock saw the Glasgow & South Western responding by rebuilding

Opposite: *Queen Mary II, King Edward* and *Duchess of Montrose* in Albert Harbour 1949.

Lucy Ashton (1888) at Princes Pier.

The Tea Room in the *Glen Rosa* (1893).

Princes Pier on a very elaborate scale in a florid Italian style. The new station and pier opened in May 1894. Among the ships built for the services from Princes Pier were the *Jupiter* of 1896 from J. & G. Thomson, Clydebank and *Mars* of 1902 from the same yard, now trading as John Brown. It was of the *Mars* that the journalist, novelist and poet J. J. Bell wrote in his *Song of a River Steamer*: a poem which admirably captures the spirit of the Clyde in the early years of this century:

> I know the Clyde in its summer pride
> And eke in its winter gloom;
> I know what it is to carry good biz
> And nothing but plenty of room;
> I know the thousands who sail for fun,
> The hundreds depending on me –
> And in the black of the night or in the blaze o' the sun
> I'm as handsome a craft as you'll see!
>
> Travellers watching my engines go,
> Folk in my fine saloon,
> Passengers pale in a Januar' gale
> Or under an August moon,
> Ladies sunning themselves on deck,
> Gents with their choice cigars –
> They all can feel they are quite genteel
> Aboard the magnificent *Mars!*

P.S. *Mars* (1902), a typical G. & S.W.R. steamer.

☝ Ocean Terminal

The Clydeport container terminal. Lines that have used this terminal include Sea Train Lines, Blue Star Line, Hapag Lloyd (Nurnberg & Koln Express). The deep water quay allows access for container ships at any state of the tide and the three container cranes on the quayside make for fast turnaround times. Weekly container ship services link Greenock with Bilbao in Spain and the French port of Le Havre. The Le Havre route, apart from servicing the French market, allows Scottish exporters and shippers good onward connections to Europe, North America and the Far East. The Ocean Terminal is also used for the increasing number of cruise liners (including *QE2*) which are now calling at the Clyde. The third important trade carried out from the terminal is the import and export of timber and other forest products such as woodpulp and plyboard. Greenock's traditional sugar trade is now also dealt with through this terminal.

Also to be seen adjacent to the Ocean Terminal is the base for Clyde Marine Motoring Company Ltd. This firm operates cruising services on the Firth and a passenger ferry service linking Greenock, Kilcreggan on the Rosneath peninsula and Helensburgh with their vessels *The Second Snark*, *Kenilworth* and *Rover*. Established in 1930 this firm has done much tendering work for Clyde-built vessels on trials and its ships have also towed various craft in and out of docks.

The Estuary Control Tower is also located at the Terminal. This serves both as the base for the Clyde Pilot service and as the centre for control of river movements between Glasgow and No. 1 buoy at the Tail of the Bank.

℞ Tail of the Bank

The River dramatically widens at this point and turns into the estuary or Firth.

In the middle of the river may be seen the wreck of the *Captayannis*. Coming into Greenock with a cargo of sugar in January 1974 she was caught in a severe gale, dragged her anchor and capsized. No attempt has been made to salvage her as she lies out of major shipping lanes. The *Captayannis* is remarkably well preserved due to her position. As her hull faces into prevailing westerly winds her superstructure remains largely undamaged.

Until the late 1960's many ships bound for Glasgow lay here awaiting the tide.

Craigendoran

The twin piers of Craigendoran, the former base of the North British Steam Packet Company (later London and North Eastern Railway – L.N.E.R.) can be seen on the Northern shore. This was opened in 1882 as an integrated rail and steamer port. The ships which used Craigendoran until 1947 were a magnificent sight with their black, white and red funnels, brown deck saloons, black hulls with two gold bands and gold leaf decoration round the paddle boxes. All these ships were named after books and characters created by Sir Walter Scott – *Talisman, Dandie Dinmont, Marmion*, etc. Particularly popular was the *Lucy Ashton*, built in 1888 by T. B. Seath at Rutherglen, which maintained the Craigendoran services during the Second World War. She survived in service until February 1949, having celebrating her Diamond Jubilee in 1948. Restricted depth of water at Craigendoran obliged the Company to continue to use shallower draft paddle steamers when other companies had moved to turbine screw steamers. *Waverley* was the last of the old L.N.E.R. ships in service when Craigendoran, her home port, closed in 1972. The last vessel to use the pier was the *Maid of Cumbrae*, built in 1953. One or two special cruises for enthusiasts have since come in for brief photo calls.

During both World Wars many Clyde steamers, including most of the Craigendoran fleet, were requisitioned for active service. Minesweeping duties occupied many Clyde steamers in both wars. Some like the *Waverley* of 1899 served in the 1914-18 War and were still serviceable enough to be called up again in 1939.

Craigendoran Pier, mid 1930's with *Waverley* (1899), *Jeanie Deans* (1931) and *Lucy Ashton* (1888).

Passengers landing from the *Redgauntlet* (1895) at Craigendoran.

Dining room, *Jeanie Deans* (1931).

Crew and passengers on deck of the *Lucy Ashton* (1888) in 1933.

Passengers boarding the *Lucy Ashton* (1888) at Roseneath.

Waverley was sunk assisting in the evacuation of the British Expeditionary Force from Dunkirk in May 1940. Other steamers performed a variety of roles – in the Second World War, for example, the *Jeanie Deans* was used as an anti-aircraft ship in the Thames Estuary and the *Talisman* was used as a headquarters ship for one of the Mulberry artificial harbours used in the Normandy D-Day landings.

Helensburgh

Helensburgh is a planned town, created in the 1770's and 1780's on the site of the tiny fishing village of Milligs. Helensburgh had of course been the original destination of Henry Bell's *Comet*, even though the new town had no pier and the *Comet's* first passengers must have had a rough and ready landing at a small slipway. A jetty was built in 1816 but this was described by the newspapers of the day as being just "a ruckle of stanes". A more serviceable pier was constructed in 1859 but this was several hundred yards walk from the railway station. The North British Railway had originally planned to build their new integrated steamer terminal at Helensburgh and submitted a formal proposal to this end in 1879. This would have involved bringing the railway line right along the Helensburgh seafront and many of the town's citizens objected to the idea of such an intrusion into their pleasant and well-ordered town. A campaign was vigorously and successfully mounted against the plan, forcing the Company to withdraw their proposal and to develop their terminal at Craigendoran instead.

Waverley approaching Helensburgh 16/4/1966 on charter, celebrating the North British Centenary. The first call since closure in the early 1950's.

Helensburgh Pier was always shallow and tidal and services from here were reduced after the development of Craigendoran, eventually being reduced to calls by the Gareloch steamer. Neil Munro, writing of the Clyde in 1907, summed up the position well:

A somewhat forlorn pier keeps Helensburgh to some extent in touch with its neighbour towns on the firth, but there is no harbour, and the bulk of the railway traffic for the coast is from Craigendoran, a station and pier at its extreme eastern boundary. The busy Greenock roadstead with its varied shipping adds to the interest of Helensburgh's days; the further lights of towns on the Firth give its nights a hint of distant festival.

The "somewhat forlorn pier" closed to scheduled steamer services in 1952 because of lack of custom and the silting up of the approaches. Services by small motor vessels continued and in 1979 the area was dredged to allow the *Waverley* to resume visits and she now calls here regularly in season.

Henry Bell, the pioneer of steam navigation, was the first Provost of Helensburgh, between 1807 and 1810. He also built and ran the Baths Inn, later the Queens Hotel, in the town. This large square building painted in a cream and ochre brown wash can still be seen approximately halfway between Craigendoran and Helensburgh pier – it has now been extended and converted into flats. The Baths Inn was the first hotel on the Clyde built to cater for the new and highly fashionable taste for sea-bathing. Bell was to be involved with the Baths Inn until his death in 1830 and afterwards his widow continued to run it until her death in 1854. A poetic guide-book to the Clyde, published in 1820, noted of Bell that:

Though infirm, yet he holds on the paths
Of Business; and here I may tell,
His House has some elegant Baths,
A commodious Inn and Hotel.

The Baths Inn was indeed the leading hotel of the area, patronised by holiday makers as well as those in search of sea-bathing, felt then to be a cure for almost everything. The novelist John Galt described the Baths Inn's facilities and clients:

When I had ate my dinner and drunk my toddy at the pleasant hotel of Helensburgh, in which there are both hot and cold baths for invalid persons, and others afflicted with rheumatics, and suchlike incomes, I went out again to take another walk, for I had plenty of time on my hands, as the steam-boat was not to sail for Glasgow until six o'clock.

A monument to Bell, erected in 1872, may be seen 100 yards West of Helensburgh pier on the sea-front. Among Helensburgh's other famous residents were John Logie Baird, the pioneer of television and the film-star of the 1930s and 40s Jack Buchanan.

Ŋ̂ Gareloch

On leaving Helensburgh, Rhu narrows and the entrance to the Gareloch can be seen. This little loch once boasted over half a dozen piers and the faithful *Lucy Ashton* provided a commuter service for local residents, bringing them to Helensburgh, Craigendoran and the train connections to Glasgow. A 7.00 a.m. departure from Garelochhead made residence on Garelochside compatible with business in Glasgow. An afternoon run down the loch at 2.00 p.m. was equally popular with shoppers coming to Helensburgh from the lochside villages. The *Lucy Ashton* was taken out of service in 1949 but had an unusual after-life, being used for two years for experimental work on the Clyde. She had most of her superstructure cut away and was fitted with two Rolls Royce jet engines and used for important, and extremely noisy, research into hull design.

The loch was once a popular haven for newly built or refitted ships to anchor and adjust their compasses. The Gareloch was also one of many sheltered areas around the Firth of Clyde which were frequently used for the laying-up of redundant merchant and naval vessels. One of Neil Munro's Para Handy stories tells of the Gareloch full of ships in the depression of the 1920s.

As the *Vital Spark*, outrageously belching sparks and cinders from fuel eked out by wood purloined some days before from a cargo of pit-props, swept round the point of Row, Para Handy gazed with wonder and adoration at the Gareloch, full of idle ships. "My word!" he exclaimed, "isn't that the splendid sight! Puts ye in mind o' a Royal Review!"

"I don't see onything Royal aboot it," growled the misanthropic engineer, Macphail. "It's a sign o' the terrible times we're livin' in. If there was freights for them boats, they wouldna be there, but dashin' roond the Horn and makin' work for people." "Of course! Of course! You must aye be contrary," said the Captain peevishly. "Nothing on earth 'll please you, ye're that parteecular. It's the way they chenerally make work for people that spoils ships for me. I like them best when they're at their moorin's. What more could ye want in the way o' a bonny spectacle than the sight o' aal them gallant vessels and them no' sailin'?"

A major shipbreaking yard was established at Faslane on the Gareloch where many great ships ended their day, including the

Cunarder *Aquitania* and the battleship HMS *Vanguard*. During the Second World War Faslane became a major military port with miles of railway sidings, and was much used for the loading of convoys for the North African campaign and the invasion of Europe. Faslane now hosts the Clyde Submarine Base, the home of the Royal Navy's Polaris and Trident nuclear submarines.

Gourock

Gourock was, in earlier years, the hub of steamer services on the Clyde. It was the headquarters of the Caledonian Steam Packet Company, founded in 1889 as a subsidiary of the Caledonian Railway. The first steamers of their fleet were the Holy Loch steamers *Meg Merrilies* and *Madge Wildfire* acquired from Campbells of Kilmun and these were added to in the first year by the *Caledonia* and *Galatea*. An active building programme continued with the *Duchess of Hamilton, Marchioness of Breadalbane* and *Marchioness of Bute* coming into service in the fleet in 1890.

The development of Gourock by the Caledonian Steam Packet Company meant that their services to the coast had leap-frogged over the Greenock base of the Glasgow & South Western Railway Company. The possibilities of the shorter and quicker firth crossings possible from Gourock made the town the principal port

Glen Sannox with *Duchess of Montrose,* off Gourock, taken from *Caledonia* in 1949.
Photo: Andrew McKechnie

Queen Elizabeth, Marchioness of Lorne *and* Duchess of Montrose *in 1946.*
Photo: Bill Young

for the Clyde. The popular character "Wee Macgreegor", created by
J. J. Bell in his stories for the *Glasgow Evening Times* in the early
years of this century, had the attractions of Greenock services and
the commercial realities of Clyde steamers explained to him by his
grandfather on Rothesay Esplanade. They are awaiting the arrival
from Glasgow of Macgreegor's mother and his grandfather says:

"Wait till ye see a boat wi' twa yellow funnels."

Clearly a reference to the yellow funnels of the Caley steamers. But
Macgreegor has his own opinions and as a good Glaswegian we
may suspect him to have developed a partiality for MacBrayne's all
the way sailings:

"I like rid funnels better nor yella yins. Whit wey is Maw comin'
in a boat wi' yella funnels?
"Yer Maw disna like the watter, an' the boats wi' yella funnels
dinna come sae faur as the boats wi' red funnels. That's jist the
wey o't, Macgreegor.

The Railway Pier in its great days could accommodate five or six
steamers but now is much less used and has partly fallen into
decay. Part of it is still used as terminal for the Gourock to Dunoon
service operated by Caledonian MacBrayne's three car ferries *Juno,*
Jupiter and *Saturn.* Sadly, the evocative and once famed sign at
Gourock railway station "To the Steamers" is no more, nor are you

likely to read press reports like this one from *The Bulletin* in July 1935:

> Traffic by the steamers from Gourock and Wemyss Bay was very heavy on Saturday, and again there were large crowds of day trippers. On Saturday the MacBrayne's steamer *Columba* for the Loch Fyne ports was packed when she arrived at Gourock and it was impossible to take any more passengers on board.

The pleasures of day trip sailings on the Clyde were offered by a variety of steamers; in July 1935 Turbine Steamers Ltd. could provide sailings on the *Queen Alexandra* to Lochranza, Pirnmill and Campbeltown and on the *King George V* to Inveraray via the Kyles of Bute at cheap day fares of 5/8d (28p.) and 7/8d (38p.) Venturing slightly further afield, Burns & Laird, at the same Glasgow Fair period, were offering a Sunday cruise by their *Lairds Isle* from Ardrossan to Bangor, County Down, with two hours ashore, for 11/- (55p.) including rail connection from Glasgow or Paisley to Ardrossan. If further inducement was needed Luncheons and High Teas could be had on board for 2/6d. (13p.)

Quite how extensive the network of steamer services and how fiercely competitive the Clyde steamer system once was is shown by the fact that at the outbreak of the First World War in 1914 there were thirty-nine steamers in commission on the river and

Transylvania (1925) with the *Caledonia* (1925) at the Tail o' the bank in 1928. They were from New York and Boston repectively, met off the US coast and crossed the Atlantic in company, with a party of 2,500 from the "Order of Scottish Clans in America".

firth. Twenty-nine of these ships were called up for Government service and the Clyde's needs were left to be covered by the remaining ten vessels. After the war, numbers built up again as ships returned from naval duties and in the later 1920s and 1930s new construction, such as the *Glen Sannox* and the *Duchess of Montrose*, came into service for the Caledonian Steam Packet Company and the *Jeanie Deans* and the diesel electric paddler *Talisman* for the L.N.E.R.

At the beginning of the Second World War in 1939 the Clyde passenger fleet numbered thirty vessels; the Craigendoran fleet of five L.N.E.R. ships, the Caledonian Steam Packet Company's nineteen vessels, MacBrayne's four Clyde-based ships and two ships – the *Dalriada* and *Davaar* of the Clyde and Campbeltown Shipping Company running between Glasgow and Campbeltown. In the Second World War many of these ships were called-up for war service and again the Clyde area was left to be served by a small, hard-worked fleet. In the post-war period numbers never regained their pre-war levels and war-time losses were not replaced. The only post war passenger steamer to be built in the classic mould was the *Waverley* in 1947, although four small motor vessels *Maid of Argyll, Maid of Ashton, Maid of Cumbrae*, and *Maid of Skelmorlie* were added in 1953 to replace older paddle steamers. Since that time new construction has been confined to car ferries.

While up until the early 1970s it was possible to sail to all parts of the Firth of Clyde from Gourock pier, today's Clyde sailings consist of the Arran car ferry from Ardrossan, the Gourock to Dunoon car ferry, the Wemyss Bay to Rothesay car ferry, all of which are operated by Caledonian MacBrayne. This company also runs the Colintraive-Rhubodach car ferry at the North end of Bute, a car ferry linking Cowal and Tarbert in Kintyre, the car ferry between Largs and Cumbrae and a car ferry service between Lochranza in Arran and Kintyre. In addition Western Ferries operate a car ferry service between McInroy's Point and Hunter's Quay while Clyde Marine Motoring offer passenger services between Gourock, Kilcreggan and Helensburgh.

Pilot boats formerly berthed at the West end of Gourock Pier and from here the *Gantock* and *Cumbrae* went out to meet those ships requiring pilotage. The radar installations on Gourock pier were part of the facilities of an outstation of the Glasgow College of Nautical Studies.

Opposite: The Fair holidays.
(photo: Argyll & Bute District Libraries)

Jupiter (1974)

The little town of Gourock has grown up along the seaside and owes much to its marine connections. The development of the town, strung out in a narrow strip along the riverside explains the local saying "a' to one side like Gourock". Gourock, once a popular holiday resort, enjoys magnificent views West and North over the Clyde to the Dunbartonshire and Argyllshire hills – how appropriate it was that Neil Munro should describe the colour of the newly painted *Vital Spark's* funnel as being :

> . . . red as gorgeous as a Gourock sunset.

Although Gourock as we see it today owes much to the coming of the railway and the steamer it is, nevertheless, an old and historic town – King James IV sailed from here in 1494 on an expedition to bring the unruly chieftains of the Western Isles under royal authority. If further claim to fame is needed Gourock is credited with the curing of the first Scottish red herring in 1688. A noted feature of Gourock is the prehistoric monolith known as "Granny Kempock". In the words of the Victorian *Ordnance Gazetteer* this stone was:

> . . . looked upon with superstitious awe. Sailors and fishermen would pace seven times around it, carrying a basketful of sea-sand and chanting an eerie strain, thereby to ensure a prosperous breeze; whilst a newly-wedded pair must also make the round of it, if they would have good luck.

The growth of industry in the towns of the Clyde, the development of tourism, the industrial growth of Glasgow itself are all closely linked to the development of steamer services on the river. In 1816, just four years after Henry Bell's *Comet* had undertaken its pioneering voyage:

. . . by the power of wind, air and steam

---

the Glasgow historian James Cleland described the dramatic changes which were already to be seen on the river.

> The public, however, having gained confidence by degrees, in a navigation, which became at once expeditious and pleasant, it was preferred to every other mode of conveyance; for the expedition of the voyage, and beauty of the scenery on the banks of the Clyde, are such, as to attract alike the attention of the man of business and pleasure; and the watering-places all along the coast, have been crowded with company beyond all former precedent, in consequence of steam conveyance. It has been calculated, that, previous to the erection of Steam-Boats, not more than fifty persons passed and re-passed from Glasgow to Greenock in one day; whereas, now it is supposed that there are from four to five hundred passes and repasses in the same period.

The "all the way" sailing as a regular and much-loved part of the life of Glasgow and the Clyde lasted from 1812 to 1969. Fortunately something of this century and half of Clyde tradition can still be experienced by the passenger on board the *Waverley* as she beats her way "doon the watter" from the centre of the city to explore the summer beauties of the Firth. Beauties which are enticingly laid out before us at Gourock as the Clyde, Glasgow's River, broadens out into the Firth of Clyde with its pattern of islands and lochs. The Victorian writer Alexander Smith described this scene in *A Boy's Poem*:

> Before us, out towards the mighty sun,
> The firth was throbbing with glad flakes of light.
> The mountains from their solitary pines
> Run down in bleating pastures to the sea;
> And round and round the yellow coasts I saw
> Each curve and bend of the delightful shore
> Hemmed with a line of villas white as foam.

Here at the Highland Boundary Fault, where the Lowlands give way to the Highlands, we must bring to an end our nostalgic look back at the life and work of the Clyde.

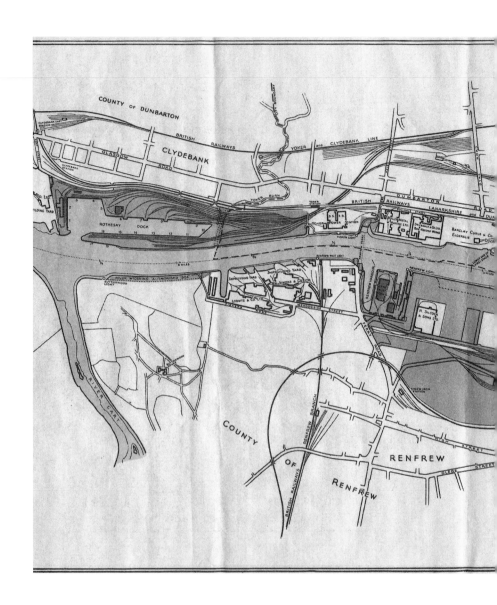

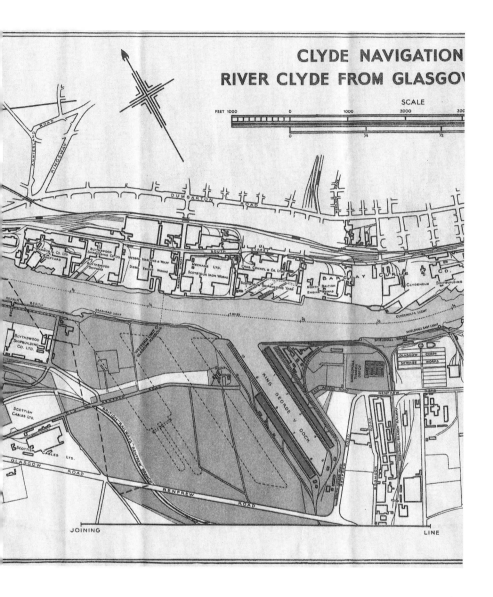

Glasgow's River from Shieldhall Wharf to Rothesay Dock.

The following clubs meet in Glasgow (winter only), welcome new members and information on their programmes and activities can be had from the addresses shown.

Clyde River Steamer Club
Founded 1932. Meets monthly. 2 magazines published per year
Contact: 67 Atholl Drive, Giffnock.

West Highland Steamer Club
Founded 1967. Meets monthly. 2 magazines published per year.
Contact: Wardiebank House, 21 Boswall Road, Edinburgh.

Coastal Cruising Association
Founded 1964. Meets monthly. 12 magazines published per year.
Contact: 15 Avondale Drive, Paisley.

Paddle Steamer Preservation Society (Scottish Branch)
Founded 1969. Meets monthly. 4 magazines published per year.
Contact: 12 Chestnut Avenue, Kilearn G63 9SJ.

Clyde Shiplovers
Founded 1932. Meets fortnightly.
Contact: 8 Airthrey Avenue, Glasgow G14 9JR.

Clyde cruises can be made with Waverley Excursions Ltd., P.S. *Waverley*, Anderston Quay, Glasgow G3 8HA.
Tel: 0141 221 8152.

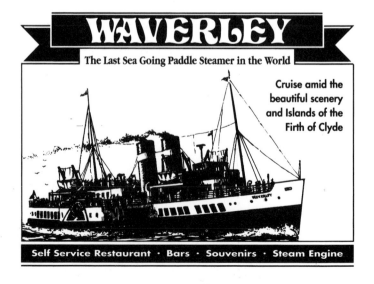

WAVERLEY

The Last Sea Going Paddle Steamer in the World

Cruise amid the beautiful scenery and Islands of the Firth of Clyde

Self Service Restaurant · Bars · Souvenirs · Steam Engine